THE CREVASSE

.

THE CREVASSE

A Critical Response to David Day's *Flaws In The Ice*

Karyn Maguire Bradford

The Erskine Press
2015

THE CREVASSE
A Critical Response to David Day's *Flaws in the Ice*

First Published 2015 by
The Erskine Press, The White House, Sandfield Lane, Eccles, Norwich NR16 2PB
WWW.ERSKINE-PRESS.COM

Text © Karyn Maguire Bradford

Introduction © Beau Riffenburgh

The moral right of the author has been asserted

A CIP catalogue record is available from the British Library

This edition © The Erskine Press
ISBN 978 1 85297 118 2

Printed and bound in Great Britain by
Barkers Print and Design Ltd, Norfolk

Douglas Mawson

Once come here, and I defy any one to be quite the same again. From the creation the silence here has been unbroken by man, and now we, a very prosaic crowd of fellows, are here for an infinitely small space of time; for a short time we shall litter the land with our tins, scrap timber, refuse, and impedimenta; for a short time we shall be travelling over the great plateau, trying to draw the veil from a fractional part of this unknown land; then the ship will return for us and we shall leave the place to its eternal silence and loneliness, a silence that may never again be broken by a human voice.

Lieutenant Belgrave Ninnis[1]

It is not the critic who counts; not the man who points out how the strong man stumbles, or where the doer of deeds could have done them better. The credit belongs to the man who is actually in the arena, whose face is marred by dust and sweat and blood; who strives valiantly; who errs, who comes short again and again, because there is no effort without error and shortcoming; but who does actually strive to do the deeds; who knows great enthusiasms, the great devotions; who spends himself in a worthy cause; who at the best knows in the end the triumph of high achievement, and who at the worst, if he fails, at least fails while daring greatly, so that his place shall never be with those cold and timid souls who neither know victory nor defeat.

Theodore Roosevelt[2]

CONTENTS

Distances and Weights

I have used miles (statute) and pounds/ounces throughout, since these are the measures used at the time and mentioned frequently in the diaries. Where I think it necessary for clarity, I have included conversions to metric measures.

Beaufort Wind Scale

Force	Description	Speed (mph)	Effect
0	Calm		May cause smoke to move from vertical
1-3	Light winds	1-12	Moves the leaves of trees
4	Moderate winds	13-17	
5	Fresh winds	18-24	Good sailing breeze, makes white caps
6	Strong winds	25-30	
7	Near gale	31-38	Sways trees and breaks small branches
8	Gale	39-46	
9	Strong gale	47-54	Dangerous for sailing vessels
10	Storm	55-63	
11	Violent Storm	64-72	Prostrates exposed trees and frail houses.
12	Hurricane	73+	

Antarctic Expeditions

Abbreviation	Name of Expedition	Leader	Vessel
NAE	National Antarctic Expedition 1901-04	Robert Falcon Scott	*Discovery*
BAE 1907	British Antarctic Expedition 1907-09	Ernest Shackleton	*Nimrod*
BAE 1910	British Antarctic Expedition 1910-13 a.k.a. Scott's Last Expedition	Robert Falcon Scott	*Terra Nova*
	Amundsen's South Pole Expedition 1910-12	Roald Amundsen	*Fram*
AAE	Australasian Antarctic Expedition 1911-14	Douglas Mawson	*Aurora*
ITAE	Imperial Trans Antarctic Expedition 1914-17	Ernest Shackleton	*Endurance* (Weddell Sea) *Aurora* (Ross Sea)
BANZARE	British Australian and New Zealand Antarctic Research Expedition	Douglas Mawson	*Discovery*

INTRODUCTION

There has long been a practice by some of those who write history or biographies to sensationalise their work, to make controversial claims, or even to fabricate details – often just to make points that will gain the attention of reviewers or the reading public. Debunking famous people can be good for sales, whether such refutations are based on facts discovered by intensive and original research or on wild supposition. Discrediting national heroes seems to have been particularly popular in the world of exploration – David Livingstone was reassessed psychologically by Oliver Ransford, Robert Falcon Scott was castigated mercilessly by Roland Huntford, Henry Morton Stanley was turned into a brutal and paranoid homosexual by Frank McLynn, and Roald Amundsen was presented as a relentless womanizer by Tor Bormann-Larsen.

Because of the legal position expressed in the old adage 'you can't libel the dead,' the great Antarctic explorer Douglas Mawson (1882–1958) has been open to attacks that he almost certainly would respond to vigorously were he still alive.

Such negative claims are often made in a search for sensational new perspectives by an author who is apparently determined to sell his book by denigrating the subject's standing.

This is not to say that Mawson was not ambitious, aloof, often difficult to deal with, and at times humourless. But David Day's account is so eager to find fault with and see the worst in Mawson that it proves not just unbalanced but a virtual caricature. The debunking that Day is so desperate to carry out is accomplished in part by regularly interpreting events, interactions, and decisions in the way that does the most harm to Mawson's reputation. But Day also attempts to achieve his purpose by steadfastly ignoring the research, publications, and conclusions of those Antarctic scholars and historians who have made more positive judgements about Mawson through the years. He also attempts to claim special knowledge gained from sources mysteriously 'hidden away for the last century' – in reality, these sources have long been available in public libraries and archives, where they have been studied by historians and enthusiasts for decades. Even Day's most damning source – the recently published diary of Cecil Madigan – was not 'long-suppressed' as claimed, since years ago I was given permission to see the original as part of my research for *Aurora* and *Racing With Death*, my two books about Mawson and the Australasian Antarctic Expedition.

Almost twenty years ago, Kevin Kenny wrote that a book was 'a peculiarly misleading mixture of speculation… and documented, undocumented, and mis-documented historical "facts".' I think the same can be said about Day's roasting of Mawson, which I believe clearly goes well beyond the boundaries of honest scholarly practice by, among other things, misrepresenting documented facts and making statements that are simply false. Because his aim is apparently to ruin Mawson's reputation, it overwhelms any historical objectivity, so the book becomes not a careful assessment of the explorer based on 'new evidence,' but rather an unpalatable effort that is fundamentally untrue.

Therefore, for those of us with a desire for historical accuracy, a passion for fair treatment of historical characters, and, admittedly, admiration for Mawson and his achievements, it is a happy turn of events that Karyn Maguire Bradford has stepped forward to defend the maligned explorer. The arguments presented in her essay are an attempt to offset the unrelentingly negative portrayal produced by Day with a more thoughtful appraisal, which will allow the reader to make a reasoned and knowledgeable assessment of Mawson as a man, a leader, an explorer, and a scientist. In each of these roles, Mawson showed himself to be a figure of substance and significance and not someone who should be lightly dismissed by a work that, though full of unsubstantiated claims, actually introduces very little new genuine evidence or historical fact. I believe that, for trying to balance the scales of historical justice, Bradford is to be sincerely thanked.

Beau Riffenburgh

1

BACKGROUND

The stories of the great Antarctic explorers have enthralled me since childhood. I first learnt about Scott and Amundsen and the race for the South Pole when such heroic tales were part of the standard course in primary school social studies. At age eleven, I was the first person to borrow a crisp new copy of *Scott's Last Expedition* from the local council library, and I devoured it from cover to cover.

My interest in Antarctica then lay dormant for quite some time, until I happened to find a copy of Roland Huntford's *Scott and Amundsen* in a local bookshop sometime in my late twenties. My passion was reawakened, and from that moment onwards I have been completely hooked. My library of books about the Antarctic explorers has expanded inexorably during the intervening years, and continues to grow with each new publication and every second-hand bookshop find.

Roland Huntford's *Scott and Amundsen* was the start of the modern iconoclastic approach to polar history. However my own academic studies, as well as half a lifetime of reading, have shown me that it is a mistake to place too much reliance on any single source, or any one point of view, when there is other evidence available. I did not accept Huntford's controversial opinion of Scott as the entire story, and I have since read many differing points of view, including the primary sources wherever possible, and made up my own mind.

Douglas Mawson and the Australasian Antarctic Expedition came to my attention as my interest spread beyond the expeditions of Scott and Amundsen, and I read further into the accounts of what is now called the 'Heroic Age' of Antarctic exploration. The story of Mawson's epic survival trek, firstly with Mertz, and ultimately alone, particularly resonated with me. I have found it to be a great source of personal inspiration and encouragement. Every time I thought something in my life was difficult, I would remind myself of what Mawson survived, and that no matter what obstacle he encountered, he *never* quit.

Any new book about Mawson would always be at the very top of my 'must read' list, so I was eager to read Dr David Day's *Flaws In The Ice*, published in 2013. However, the completely negative picture that Day presents came as a great shock, since it was utterly at odds with everything that I thought I knew about Mawson, and the Australasian Antarctic Expedition. Day hardly makes a single positive comment about either the man, or his achievements. Instead he takes every possible opportunity for criticism. The disrespect he shows for Mawson starts subtly even before the preface, when the list of expedition members does not give Mawson his correct title of 'Dr', when others are given that courtesy.

After reading *Flaws In The Ice* I understood what Scott's admirers had felt when *Scott and Amundsen* was first published. This inspired me to return to Mawson's diary and his published account once more, and review them in the light of the recently published diaries of expedition members Cecil Madigan, John Hunter, Frank Stillwell and Belgrave Ninnis, as well as Day's extremely critical analysis. Could everything I had previously read, and the opinion I had formed, be so wrong? I have questioned and re-examined my pre-conceived ideas about Mawson.

In this essay I will analyse some of the most damning criticisms Day makes of Mawson, and present a contrasting point of view based on evidence from many sources. Day also discusses Mawson's behaviour and activities following the expedition and during the First World War. My comments and analysis will concentrate entirely on his Antarctic expeditions.

Please bear in mind as you read this essay, that I am an amateur historian, not a professional academic or researcher. My research has therefore focused on published materials, and a limited amount of the unpublished material held at the Mitchell Library.

I do not intend to re-tell the story of the expedition and the dramatic events that occurred during Mawson's Far Eastern sledging journey. That has been done many times, by writers far better than me. I will assume that anyone sufficiently interested in Mawson to be reading this essay will already be aware of the history. If by some chance this is not the case, please do not spoil your enjoyment of this truly great story; stop reading this now, and see the following for my suggestions of narrative accounts of the expedition to read first.

If you are new to the story of Mawson and the AAE:

If this is your first encounter with Mawson, please do not read this essay until you have read at least one full account of the Expedition.

For a popular account, I would suggest any of the following:

Racing With Death by Beau Riffenburgh

This Accursed Land by Lennard Bickel

Mawson: And the Ice Men of the Heroic Age: Scott, Shackleton and Amundsen by Peter Fitzsimons

Alone on the Ice by David Roberts

For a more academic account, the definitive work on the expedition is:

Aurora: Douglas Mawson and the Australian Antarctic Expedition 1911-14 by Beau Riffenburgh

Ideally, you should also read *Flaws In The Ice* by David Day, before reading this essay.

Publication details for all of the above books are in the Bibliography.

2

CONSPIRACIES AND COVER-UPS?

In his introduction Dr David Day says that newly published diaries, released to coincide with the centenary of the expedition, shed new light and made "a more complete portrait of Mawson and a more balanced assessment of the expedition" possible.[3]

Day is correct in saying that previously published accounts have not differed substantially from the information that Mawson himself wrote in his published account of the expedition *The Home Of The Blizzard*, and his diaries which were edited and published in 1988, thirty years after his death, and after all of the other expedition members had also died. History is usually written by the victors, and expedition books, the immediate 'official' versions at least, are written by the leaders who have put such enormous efforts into organising and running these enterprises, and put their reputations on the line. They also usually have the contractual rights, indeed, frequently a contractual obligation, to write and publish such a book. Expedition leaders naturally have a vested interest in presenting themselves and their expedition in the most favourable light. Does any reader seriously expect otherwise?

This is particularly true of accounts from the 19th and early 20th centuries when it was just 'not the done thing' to air your dirty laundry in public. Interpersonal conflict was simply not mentioned in most of the early accounts; everyone supposedly got along famously and behaved like perfect gentlemen from start to finish; and the whole show was just 'top-hole', to coin a phrase common at that time. Readers today understand the differences between the prevailing cultures of the early 20th century and of today, and apply common sense and a dash of modern sensibility to read between the lines, even if just a little, to imagine what life on an expedition in Antarctica during the 'heroic age' might *really* have been like. In fact, the AAE was unusual for its time, since Mawson did not completely cover up the mental breakdown of Jeffryes during the second winter in his official published account of the expedition.[4] That is surely an indication of exactly how bad that situation was.

The other accounts published by members of the expedition, Frank Hurley's *Argonauts of the South (1925)*, and Charles Laseron's *South With Mawson* (1947), are also both highly favourable to Mawson. Both of these accounts were published well before the modern trend towards 'warts and all' brutally honest accounts, but that does not mean that they are not the genuine opinions of their authors. It is an insult to these men to entirely discount these works as being less than accurate, or not their genuine opinions, simply because they are favourable to Mawson.

Day is not correct, however, in saying that many expedition diaries and materials have been "hidden away", which implies that there is some sort of vast conspiracy in place by the secret pro-Mawson faction to keep these documents away from public view, because they are detrimental to Mawson's hero status.[5] In Australia at least, this is simply not true. The vast majority of the archival materials and original diaries from the expedition are in public hands in state and national libraries and archives. The significant document holdings from the AAE at the Mitchell Library in New South Wales are available to any member of the public who is sufficiently interested to obtain a Special Collections Library Card and asks to see them.

Also of note is that the diary of Belgrave Ninnis, which Day described as remaining "under wraps at the Scott Polar Research Institute"[6] has recently been co-edited by Alan Mornement, a descendant of the Ninnis family, and polar historian Beau Riffenburgh. This diary was published in 2014, after the release of Day's *Flaws In The Ice*.

Not all the expedition materials in Australia have been publicly available, and Cecil Madigan's diary from the AAE had been the notable exception for many years. It was privately held by the Madigan family until its publication in 2012.[7]

Day presents these new points of view, especially Madigan's—the man most strongly critical of Mawson—as if they are the newly revealed absolute truth, and therefore that everything preceding them is wrong. Rather than Mawson's version, Day now asks us to accept what is essentially Madigan's version, as the true story. In fact, both versions represent just one individual's point of view, and neither is necessarily any more or less valid than the other. Day does not really give us a "more balanced approach", but rather the story from a perspective that seems to entirely dismiss Mawson's point of view.

I do not think Day adequately addresses the following questions: Are diaries reliable documents on which to **solely** make judgements about figures of historical importance? Who was Cecil Madigan and what do his diaries reveal about his personality? Why did he have such a poor opinion of Mawson, and was that opinion either reasonable, or justified, under the circumstances?

The truth presently lies somewhere at the bottom of the gaping crevasse between these two opposing viewpoints.

3

DIARIES AS SOURCE MATERIAL

There are three sides to every story, your side, my side, and the truth. And no-one is lying. Memories shared serve each differently.[8]

We each filter everything we see, hear and experience through the lens of our own unique personality, our established attitudes, and existing memories. All of us have probably experienced a situation where two people have an entirely different recall or interpretation of the same event. We all tend to hear, see, and more importantly, remember, only what suits our own world view and preconceived ideas, and this is part of the reason why supposed 'eyewitness' testimony can be so unreliable.

One of the greatest living polar explorers, Sir Ranulph Fiennes, veteran of many expeditions, had this to say about expedition diaries in his recently published book *Cold*: "Diaries on expeditions are often minefields of overreaction,"[9] and further, referring to a member of his expedition:

his diary saw the expedition through his eyes, and my diary through mine, and naturally and inevitably we interpreted events differently, and equally our entries could also be read in a variety of ways.[10]

Expedition diaries are extremely interesting primary accounts, and they undoubtedly give us a great deal of useful first-hand information. Sometimes they can make readers feel like they are almost present with the writer in that unique place and time. However, diaries should also be viewed with a degree of caution. A diary presents only that individual person's opinion and their personal interpretation and recall of events. The circumstances of their writing, and that individual's bias, must therefore be taken into consideration. Additionally, diaries represent, if not the total immediacy of new media such as Twitter, a relatively immediate account, which may not necessarily be the considered opinion of the author. For example, an entry may have been dashed off straight away while the writer is in a heightened emotional state, and not after a period of thought and reflection. Most of the time, we are unable to tell if this might have been the case.

When looking at a historical event such as the AAE, where there were eighteen participants in the main party of the expedition, several of whom kept diaries, then we must consider as many of those points of view as we possibly can, and try to understand the consensus. We can observe where individual views differ significantly from those of the majority, and attempt to understand why that might be the case.

I believe that Day has focussed overmuch on Madigan's strong criticisms of Mawson, and has not sufficiently analysed Madigan's possible bias and motivation.

4

THE AAE DIARIES IN CONTEXT

The Mawson's Huts Foundation has created a replica of the Huts as a museum in downtown Hobart, and many visitors seem to remark on how very small it is.[11] The main Winter Quarters Hut at Commonwealth Bay was 576 square feet (53.5 square metres), with a workshop added of 288 square feet (26.76 square metres). The workshop was originally intended to be the living hut of a separate expedition base, but when a location to land that party could not be found, the two huts were combined into one. To put these dimensions into perspective, the living hut was smaller than my kitchen/family living room, and the workshop was smaller than a double garage.

This very small space was home for the 18 men present for the first year of the expedition. There was no privacy at all for the men; Mawson was the only one who had a small cubicle. There was no bathroom, and just one toilet. Everyone got to have a decent bath only when they were on 'night watch' on rotation, once every 18 nights. Each man had his bunk, and there was one communal table just big enough to seat everyone. There were no comfy chairs to relax in, no pool table, nowhere else to go, except outside, and that was only possible when the appalling wind relented for long enough.[12]

The expedition had unknowingly landed in a part of Antarctica where weather conditions were significantly worse than the previously explored Ross Sea area. For example, Ninnis reports that for the month of July, the *worst* wind recorded in on the Shackleton expedition in 1908 corresponded with the AAE's *calmest*[13] day. The expedition was completely isolated from the rest of the world. During the first year, attempts to communicate using their wireless equipment via the relay station that the expedition had established at Macquarie Island were unsuccessful. Repeated attempts to raise the antenna masts high enough had failed due to the extremely high winds. However, wireless communications were established during the second year. It is something to bear in mind that had the *Aurora* not made it back to Australia, no one would have known where the two parties of the expedition had been landed, or indeed, whether they had landed at all or had been lost at sea.

All of these men were living together in a situation of prolonged stress, overcrowding, almost total lack of privacy, and a level of risk and isolation that would be completely unthinkable today. Living in such conditions would try the patience of any saint.

The literature of polar exploration, survival situations, space exploration, and other cases of enforced close confinement are full of stories of extreme interpersonal conflict, groups dividing into factions, even physical attacks and murders are not unknown in such circumstances.[14] Dr Des Lugg, head of polar medicine for the Australian Antarctic Division from 1962 to 2001, developed a 'Rule of Ten', which states that responses to interpersonal issues in a polar environment will be ten times stronger than is considered normal or appropriate in the outside world.[15]

In reality, it was therefore completely and utterly *normal* that tempers sometimes frayed, and that there was occasional conflict and discontent between the men, and between the men and their leader. Can any of us today even imagine living with their manager 24 hours per day, in such a small space, with 16 other people who are relative strangers at the outset, with the wind howling continuously, with no mobile devices, and no outside communication, for a year—and never having a disagreement with anyone, or feeling resentful about being criticised by the boss, or being told what to do? I certainly cannot. Antarctic expeditions today are still psychologically stressful, and conditions now are immeasurably better than they were in 1912.

To maintain a veneer of civility, the most likely place, and the only socially acceptable place, for anyone on the AAE to vent their frustration was in their private diary. Many of them probably never thought that their diary might be published, or even read, by anyone at all except their closest family and friends. We should therefore expect that their diaries might contain their immediate impressions, and unfiltered opinions. Some of these could be hasty and ill-considered views, or even downright mean and nasty comments that the writer in all probability would never have actually voiced, and might later regret.

What is really much more remarkable is that there seems to have been relatively little conflict, in the first year of the expedition at least, and many members reported the group as being a generally happy and harmonious one, in spite of the utterly appalling conditions. Even if you partially discount the favourable comments in Laseron and Hurley's published accounts as being products of the publication standards of their times, the recently released diaries also contain illuminating comments.

John Hunter, the expedition biologist, wrote:
> *But despite the confinement in the hut we are quite happy. There is never a bad word or quarrel in fact if anyone becomes at all turbulent he is laughed at by the others. Not boasting in any way, yet I do not think that a better tempered & more even minded lot of men could have been chosen.*[16]

Archibald McLean, Chief Medical Officer wrote:
> *We have read in other books eg Dr Cook's of the dreary dismal Antarctic*

night, but here in Adelie Land our jolly crowd of 18 laugh melancholy to scorn.[17]

Belgrave Ninnis wrote:

> *It would be an eyeopener to those who write about the gloom and ghastly monotony of the Polar Winter, if the[y] witnessed us roaring with mirth over childish jokes. No melancholy here, and no reason for it.*[18]

These are comments that Day does not highlight in his book. Of course, this is not the entire opinion of these men. Even Hunter, who seems to have been optimistic and positive most of the time, certainly mentions some problems and disputes and also makes both critical and favourable comments about Mawson, some of which will be discussed later.

Hunter's concluding remarks on leaving Commonwealth Bay include the following:

> *It has been the makings of me personally and of the others I must say the same, at least some of them; some came down as boys; they are going back as men; men in the true sense of the word; men that you will not find anywhere and as our leader says, men that have made the British nation what it is.*[19]

This sounds all very gung-ho and patriotic, but if the negative comments of some expedition members are valid, then the positive comments of others must be regarded as being no less genuine, and equally valid.

5

CECIL MADIGAN, THE MAN AND HIS DIARY

Cecil Madigan's diary tells us just as much about the man himself as it does about Mawson, and the picture is not necessarily an entirely pleasant or straightforward one. However this is an impression gained more from reading the diary in its entirety, than from reading Day's *Flaws In The Ice*.

At the start of the expedition Madigan was 22 years old, recently graduated from the University of Adelaide, and had been awarded a Rhodes Scholarship to study at Oxford. He was in love with Wynnis Wollaston, and although not formally engaged, clearly intended to marry her. To top it off, he was selected for this prestigious expedition. He was doing well, and it is clear from reading the diary that he was very pleased with himself, almost insufferably so. To me, he gives the impression of being a quite arrogant and supremely confident young man. However, we must remember that this is his private diary, and so the writer will inevitably appear to be more self-centred than is really the case.

From the outset, he is critical of Mawson, and disappointed with the other members of the expedition since they were "very young and inexperienced".[20] Many of them certainly were young and inexperienced, Madigan himself belonged firmly in that category. Madigan said of Frank Wild, "I was glad to see a capable looking member at last".[21] This is Frank Wild, who, along with Shackleton, was one of the men who currently held the 'furthest south' record. Do these comments indicate a young man with an over-developed sense of his own superiority?

Madigan also gives indications of being a snob, he calls Hannam "fat and commonplace and rude", "a coarse bore", and Hurley "a repetition of Hannam".[22] These were two of the men who were not from a university background. Madigan did later change his mind somewhat later in the expedition, about Hannam at least.

Madigan was clearly eager for praise and delighted in reporting that Captain Davis said he was as good as many of the sailors at steering the ship.[23] He liked to think he was "the best" at everything he did, whether that was steering the ship, tying sailor's knots or shooting targets.

Most worrying is Madigan's very frequent mentions of moodiness and depression. On 26 May 1912 he wrote:

> *these moods are a blight on my otherwise pleasant existence, they are a*

kind of malignant blues which render me morose, rude, unsociable, peevish and other entirely unreasonable and beastly adjectives.[24]

Madigan was clearly self-aware enough to recognise this tendency in himself. However, had Mawson known about his temperament, it is probable that this would not have been the kind of personality he would want on the team when heading into unknown parts of the Antarctic for at least a year and possibly longer. It is unlikely that anyone who showed such tendencies would make it through to selection for an Antarctic expedition today. However, a great deal more is known of psychology now, and of the psychological pressures imposed by long Antarctic expeditions in particular. Extensive personality testing was not available in 1911, whereas it is now a standard part of the expedition selection process.[25]

Madigan was also extremely sensitive to criticism, and reports on 5 April 1912 and several other occasions, that criticism from Mawson put him into one of his depressive moods.

Exceedingly depressed, one of the moods of which I always feel thoroughly ashamed, and never seem able to cure myself. Started by some words of 'Dux Ipse', which I should not have taken to heart.[26]

Not all of Madigan's comments about Mawson are negative, but the positives are rare. On 23 October 1912 he says "I get on very well with the Old Man, I like him very much, though very few do, I fear".[27] Madigan was pleased that Mawson allowed him to take a considerable quantity of wholemeal sledging biscuit on his journey, since he disliked Plasmon biscuit. "This wholemeal is taken especially for me, which was very nice of the Old Man."[28]

Unfortunately, what might have been simmering dissatisfaction with Mawson before the major sledging journeys, reached boiling point when Mawson struggled back to the hut alone just hours after the ship had left. Madigan was now dealing not only with his deep personal grief due to the deaths of two men who had become his close friends, but he was stuck in the place he had come to loathe for a second year. Madigan had agreed to stay and lead the relief party, reluctantly, from his own account. "I did what I thought my duty to the Expedition and my lost comrades."[29]

No matter what Madigan's motivation for agreeing to remain, it was a courageous thing to do, since he would have been required to launch another sledge journey almost immediately to search for Mawson. It was late in the summer by this time, and sledging conditions would likely have become increasingly difficult. This was a prospect he clearly did not relish, "I thank God I do not have to go and search."[30]

For Madigan, the timing of Mawson's return was simply appalling, and while he does not state or even imply (in my reading, at least) that any of it was a deliberate act on Mawson's part, Madigan appears unable to come to terms with it.[31]

Madigan seems to have been completely and utterly embittered by these circumstances. He was concerned that he was wasting one of the best years of his, and his girlfriend's life; that he might lose the Rhodes Scholarship; in short, that his entire life and his future hopes were totally ruined by Mawson's late return, and his own acceptance of the appointment to command the relief party. From this time on, it seems that Mawson could do nothing right in Madigan's eyes.

It is also possible that Madigan may have found the deaths of his friends more than usually distressing. Outside of wartime, the death of two close friends is not something that most young men, in normal circumstances, have to deal with at the age of 23. Ninnis, Mertz, Madigan and Bickerton, the four residents of the area of the Hut dubbed "Hyde Park Corner" had developed a strong bond, and now two of them were dead. I feel that it is also possible that Madigan may have finally started to realise how close he had personally come to death, or to leading his men to their deaths, on several occasions during his own sledging journeys. He had fallen down a crevasse to the length of his rope, and been rescued, as had Correll in his party. He had come close to not finding his tent on 22 November 1912 after climbing Aurora Peak and returning in bad weather. He had travelled for a substantial distance across sea ice without even realising it in the first instance.[32] He had cut his supplies fine and come close to not being able to find a depot. In short, he himself had taken similar risks to Mawson, but he had luckily come out on the right side of the very fine line between life and death – between success and failure – in Antarctica. I suspect that he could have come to the harsh realisation that "there, but for the grace of God, go I."

Madigan's first diary entry after Mawson's return, dated 13 February 1913 is interesting to examine. It is long, at nearly two full pages as published, but no diary entries had been made since his return to the Huts on 16 January 1913. Madigan summarises the events of the intervening period, details his grief for his friends, but makes absolutely no mention of any sympathy for what Mawson had endured, or concern for his condition.

In contrast Hunter, who had departed on the *Aurora*, on the day of Mawson's return, and with the benefit of only the most basic information about what had happened to Mawson gained from the wireless message to the ship, wrote: "but what a time our leader must have had coming back by himself; what a time he must have had".[33] Stillwell, in the same situation wrote, "My God, what terrific suffering there has been!"[34]

McLean, who, like Madigan, had heard the full story and witnessed Mawson's condition wrote:

> It was an awful tale he had to tell—a series of tragic events, which had meant the lives of Ninnis and Mertz and a desperate fight for life by himself.[35]

Mawson is likely to have been aware of Madigan's bitter feelings, at least to some degree, and his later offer to help with Madigan's studies may have been his attempt at offering some recompense, and the only thing he could do in the circumstances. While Madigan initially thought this was "very good of him" he later seems to have rebuffed it somewhat, not wanting to be a slave to study.[36] However, Madigan did eventually complete some study with Mawson during the second winter.[37]

Madigan's previously reported bouts of depression appear to become worse, and during this period he also reported apparently unexplained positive mood swings.

I don't know why, these moods take me about once a month. I seem able to see things cheerfully, when I know everything is wretched.[38]

His arguments with Mawson increase. On 16 April 1913 Madigan reports a major argument with Mawson,

It has come to it at last, I have had a row with Mawson. He has annoyed me excessively for months and today he used words to me I won't take from anyone, and I told him so.[39]

Yet Mawson makes no mention of this in his diary. In fact Mawson states not long after this that he thinks Madigan, along with Bage and Hodgeman are doing the best work for the expedition.[40] Alarmingly, Madigan may have taken out some of his frustrations on the dogs, reporting very harsh treatment in the name of discipline. For example, on 23 April 1913 he says that he "thrashed every dog with an axe handle...I beat them to a standstill" after they had seriously injured one of their number and Madigan had to put it down.[41]

By June Madigan reports further arguments, having lost all respect for Mawson, and finally having decided that he will not speak to Mawson unless it is absolutely necessary, such as when he is spoken to.[42] Again there is no mention of any conflict in Mawson's diary.

Madigan was also concerned that Mawson's sledging journey had been a failure, while his coastal exploration had been a far better effort, yet Mawson was putting his own "before the limelight as the principal journey". Madigan thought his journey was superior in every respect;

He only saw the coast I did, visited no rocks, has no reliable astronomical observations, and in fact his work is absolutely of no value after mine.[43]

Madigan does have a valid point – one common to many people in a subordinate position in any field of endeavour. Mawson's journey did fail to meet its objective, and may have produced very little of consequence, even if it had *not* been overtaken by disaster. Mawson was only a few days short of the day on which he would have had to turn around anyway, and was still 50 miles short of the target distance. Although he may well have reached his goal if the tragedy had not occurred, and the weather had been good, he would not have had much time in which to do any serious work or travel any further. However, that is the nature of exploration. Sometimes you have to go to a place to find that it holds nothing of any great interest. Mawson was the leader of the expedition, and the author of the official expedition account. Given the dramatic nature of the events of *his* sledge journey, it is hardly surprising that it would form the centrepiece of the expedition narrative.

What we must consider is whether or not Madigan's criticisms of Mawson are either reasonable or justified in the circumstances? It is certainly possible to sympathise with Madigan, and understand why he felt as he did. However, some of his reactions appear particularly extreme. His response to the situation may be a severe demonstration of Dr Lugg's "Rule of Ten", or it may be something more.

In the first year of the expedition his comments seem to me to be nothing out of the ordinary for an Antarctic expedition. They are the normal complaints that any young man might have about his leader, especially a leader he does not seem to hold in particularly high regard, and with whom he has been living in close quarters for the better part of a year.

Everything changes in the second year. Mawson's return seemed to take the relief party by surprise; all hope of survivors appeared to have been lost. Madigan immediately surrendered all semblance of leadership to Mawson, even though Mawson was probably not in any fit state, either physically or mentally, to take charge in any meaningful way. The result appears to have been something of a leadership vacuum. Everyone seemed to be pinning their hopes on the possibility that *Aurora* might still be able to get back and pick them up, and not knowing whether to pack up again, or settle in for another year. There was a complete lack of structured activity, and even the regular night watch position (essential for safety) and cooking rota was abandoned and not re-instituted until early March. There was no longer the excitement and novelty of the first year, and malaise set in. Mawson was a firm believer in hard continuous work preventing polar depression, and was criticised severely for it by some of the men in the first year, Whetter in particular. The events of this second year of the expedition show the value of his methods.[44]

From this time onwards Mawson seems to become the focus of all of Madigan's frustration. Madigan is particularly upset by Mawson's domination of use of the wireless for 'official expedition' purposes and his own personal messages, while allowing few opportunities for the men to send a personal message of their own, and then telling them that they would have to pay for it. This was both inconsiderate and mean on Mawson's part, although his fixation with costs is understandable to a degree.[45]

Clearly Madigan was embittered, grieving, and lacking direction and purpose during the early months of 1913. On top of that, Mawson's self – rescue had robbed his sacrifice in remaining behind of its noble purpose. Could

Madigan's previously reported depressive moods have been developing into something far worse as a result? This is a possibility that I believe should be seriously considered, especially since he also reports unexplained positive mood swings during this time. I suggest that he could possibly have been suffering clinical depression or bipolar disorder.[46] A professional psychological assessment would be valuable.

If Madigan *was* ill, he seems to have either kept it well hidden, or it did not develop until the second year of the expedition. Hunter describes him as "one of the best liked" and a "jovial spirit",[47] but Hunter was not there for the second year.

The most comprehensive modern account of the AAE is *Aurora* by Beau Riffenburgh.[48] This was written before the publication of Madigan's diary, and although Riffenburgh was permitted to read the original diary, he was not allowed to quote from it, only from the privately published family history written by Madigan's son.[49] Riffenburgh does not go so far as to suggest that Madigan may have been ill, just terribly unhappy, but he does state:

> *Whether Madigan's negative assessments were recorded in his periods of extreme unhappiness or not, his overall verdict - like many of his comments about the second year- is of questionable validity because it differs so greatly from those of the others at Winter Quarters.*[50]

Madigan's focus moves away from Mawson somewhat from July 1913 onwards, once it becomes clear that Jeffryes is very seriously disturbed indeed. Many of his diary entries now centre on Jeffryes' behaviour and the efforts of Madigan and the others to deal with him. I believe that it is possible that Jeffryes illness gave all of the men something new to focus on during this very difficult time, it may have drawn them together again with a united purpose, and may ultimately have led to an improvement in Madigan's state of mind.

Madigan's possibly fragile psychological state during the first half of 1913 means that the comments he makes about Mawson in this period must be considered in this light. The extremely critical comments written at that time may not be what an objective observer would consider to be entirely fair, reasonable, or justified.

Madigan frequently expressed concern that Mawson was claiming all the credit for the expedition and the work done – "in this show it is Mawson first and the rest nowhere."[51] He may have been humbled somewhat by the official reception of the explorers in Adelaide upon their return, when his own decision to remain in command of the relief party was singled out for praise by Lord Denman, the Governor General in his speech:

> *Another rather fine instance of that spirit might be mentioned. Mr. Cecil Madigan (cheers)-had had an opportunity of coming back with Captain Davis last year to take up the Rhodes Scholarship, but he had preferred to stay behind, because he thought he could be of use to the expedition.*

(Cheers.) He felt sure the trustees of the Rhodes funds would still give Mr. Madigan an opportunity to take up the scholarship in due course. (Cheers.) His Excellency Sir Samuel Way told him that the trustees had just telegraphed to say they would do so-(cheers)-and, further, that they were proud of what Mr. Madigan had done.[52]

Madigan's relationship with Mawson in later years is puzzling. Despite the fact that he apparently completely loathed Mawson during the later part of the expedition, in 1922, after an appointment as assistant government geologist in Sudan, when he returned to Australia he took up a position at Adelaide University under Mawson, who by that time was Professor of Geology. Madigan worked in that position until his death in 1947.[53] Surely if his feelings towards Mawson remained the same as those expressed in his diaries during the first half of 1913, he would have found it intolerable to work with him, and sought a position elsewhere.

Perhaps the fact that in the intervening years everything that Madigan had wanted – and had been so concerned about losing – had eventually come to pass, may have soothed his earlier feelings, at least to some degree. Madigan did take up the Rhodes Scholarship, which had been kept available for him, and finished his education at Oxford, even though it was further interrupted by the War. He did marry his beloved Wynn, and they eventually had five children. Perhaps he had also matured, or had been tempered, by both his Antarctic and war experiences.

While Madigan's ill feelings towards Mawson may never have been entirely resolved, the two men appear to have at least been able to tolerate one another well enough to work together. In 1927 they went on expedition together into the West McDonnell ranges by motor car, and subsequently published a joint paper.[54]

In 1928 when reports began to appear in the press of Mawson mounting another expedition to Antarctica, Madigan is reported as saying he would go with Mawson if there were a position available. Later reports indicate that Madigan *was* offered a position on the expedition, but he ultimately declined it. That was certainly understandable, since it was a ship-based expedition, and there would not have been a great deal of work for a second geologist. Madigan is also reported as giving speeches in support of the Expedition, and was included in the first welcoming party to board the *Discovery* on its return, along with Mawson's wife and daughters.[55]

A relatively recent (1990) analysis of Madigan's career, written by men who were students of both Mawson and Madigan, has stated:

Madigan was a natural leader and as the years passed he found irksome his position as second in command to Mawson, himself also a striking personality. Perhaps inevitably, an element of tension developed between them. As a departmental staff of only two for much of their joint careers, their respective roles were in some measure resolved, particularly in respect of their research areas, when Madigan elected to concentrate his energies on central Australia and on the problems posed by sand ridges.[56]

These former students may not have been aware that the tensions between Mawson and Madigan had a much earlier origin.

6

Who was Responsible for the Deaths of Ninnis and Mertz?

While most historians ascribe the deaths of the two men to bad luck, my re-examination of the existing evidence and a reading of the new evidence, reveals that their deaths were caused by Mawson's relative inexperience, overweening ambition, and poor decision making.[57]

These are serious accusations from Day, so I would like to consider them point by point.

Firstly, was Mawson "relatively inexperienced"?   Relative to whom, we must ask?

In 1911 there had only been only *four* significant sledging journeys on the Antarctic continent, and just *eleven* men had any degree of experience at all of overland travel in this part of the world:

1900/3	Scott, Wilson, Shackleton	Furthest South	960 miles return including relays
1903	Scott, Evans, Lashly	Ferrar Glacier	700 miles estimated
1908/9	Shackleton, Wild, Marshall, Adams	Furthest South	1700 miles return
1908/9	David, Mawson, McKay	South Magnetic Pole Area	1260 miles including relays.[58]

Individual rank in order of distance sledged by 1911:

1	Shackleton	2660 miles
2	Wild, Marshall & Adams	1700 miles
3	Scott	1660 miles
4	*Mawson*, David & McKay	1260 miles
5	Wilson	960 miles
6	PO Edgar Evans & Lashly	700 miles

If we wished to mount a primarily Australian expedition to Antarctica, who were the likely candidates for this job to lead the AAE?

Mawson:

Had already been to Antarctica on the BAE with Shackleton, and participated in one of the four major journeys, over a wide range of terrain conditions. This journey set the record for longest *unsupported* sledge journey in Antarctica. Prior to that he had completed a survey of Vanuatu, and had recently been awarded his Doctor of Science degree by Adelaide University.

Amundsen:

Not British or Australian. Was already engaged in conducting his own expedition, and therefore not available. However, Mawson had more experience in polar travel in 1911 than Amundsen did when he set out to lead the expedition to navigate the North West Passage on *Gjoa* in 1903. At that time Amundsen had wintered in Antarctica on the *Belgica* trapped in the ice, but had not set foot on the continent, and had done no polar travel of any significance in either the Arctic or Antarctic. He was however, a qualified master mariner.

Scott:

He also had his own expedition underway at that time, so was also unavailable. Scott also had had previous Antarctic experience as the leader of the *Discovery* expedition, a great deal of hard won sledging experience as a member of two of the four major journeys. However Mawson had significantly more experience at the start of the AAE than Scott did when he was appointed to lead the *Discovery* expedition (NAE 1901). At that time Scott, while qualified for naval command, had not been anywhere near either the Arctic or Antarctic, or done any travel over ice.

Shackleton:

Had the greatest Antarctic sledging experience at that time and holder of the Furthest South record, but he had withdrawn from organising the expedition. Shackleton had been a member of Scott's *Discovery* expedition and subsequently led his own BAE 1907. Mawson's experience in 1911 was significantly greater than Shackleton's was at the time he set out as leader of the BAE in 1907.

Mawson did have considerable contact with both Scott and Shackleton during the planning of the expedition. Mawson approached Scott, asking him to land himself and a small party at Cape Adare for exploration to the west as part of his overall expedition. Scott was not interested in Mawson's plan at that stage, he was focused almost entirely on the Pole, and offered Mawson a place in his South Pole party instead. Mawson rejected that, stating that he would only go with Scott as Chief Scientist, and since that position was already filled by Wilson "I would not dream of making the suggestion".[59] Shackleton initially supported Mawson's plans and offered to assist with raising funds.

Subsequently, he seems to have wanted to take the expedition over and run it himself with Mawson as Chief Scientist, but eventually he withdrew and agreed to support Mawson.[60]

Who else was available in 1911 to lead the AAE, preferably someone who might have some connection to Australia?

Wild:
> Not Australian, but veteran of expeditions under both Scott and Shackleton. He had already been recruited by Mawson as a base leader for the AAE.

Edgeworth David:
> At 53 years of age, too old for an active part in the expedition. He was already taking a vital back of house role.

Louis Bernacchi:
> He was an Australian physicist who had also been on two Antarctic expeditions, but neither as leader, and had done no significant sledging. He does not appear to have come under consideration.

Mawson had less experience in 1911 than Amundsen, Scott and Shackleton did as of that date, but more experience than any of those men had at the time of their respective first appointments as an expedition leader.

If there was going to be any sort of predominantly Australian expedition, Mawson was the most qualified and experienced candidate available for the job. For every expedition leader, there has to be a point at which he has no previous expedition leadership experience. The AAE was Mawson's.

Secondly, did Mawson suffer from "overweening ambition"?

The AAE was certainly an ambitious and innovative project for its time – four planned bases, three on the Antarctic continent covering many hundreds of miles of previously unexplored territory, and a fourth on Macquarie Island to provide wireless communication with Australia. Mawson also planned to attempt to use aerial reconnaissance, a mere seven years after the Wright brothers' first flight.

Mawson did manage to get enough support and funding in Australia, New Zealand, and the United Kingdom to enable him to proceed with his program, and I do not think that the extraordinary difficulty of achieving that should be underestimated. Like most British expeditions, there was still considerable debt to be paid when the expedition sailed. Mawson needed the expected return from the published book, planned lecture tour, and film of the expedition to pay this debt, and pay the men. However, as is commonly said, plans rarely survive first contact with the enemy, or in this case, Antarctica.

The number of land bases was reduced from four to three, but only because a suitable landing site on that unexplored coast of Antarctica could not be found in the available time. When a single site was found at Commonwealth

Bay, two of the three bases originally planned for the Antarctic continent were combined into one. The aeroplane had crashed before it even left Australia, so its use was limited to that of a mechanical sledge puller, which Mawson called an 'air tractor'. Wireless communications were not successfully established in the first year, due to the inability to erect and maintain the masts in the extreme wind conditions prevalent at Commonwealth Bay. However, the rest of Mawson's program was implemented, and most of it was completed broadly in accordance with the plans. Since the only parts of the overall plan that were not successful were the third land base and the aircraft, that would hardly seem to be a case of Mawson's ambition overreaching his ability to organise and execute his wide-ranging expedition.

Within each of the Antarctic land bases, Mawson's plan called for sledge journeys to investigate and explore as much as possible of the surrounding regions. At Frank Wild's western base, he and his men undertook two major journeys to the east and west of the base, and three shorter depot laying journeys. Mawson's larger group mounted three preliminary journeys of short duration, severely limited by dangerous wind conditions, followed by three major, and two shorter sledging journeys during the main part of the summer season of 1912/13. In all of these sledge journeys, there was only one that experienced difficulties other than those expected under the prevailing wind and weather conditions. This indicates to me that the expedition as a whole was not either under-resourced or inappropriately equipped (in accordance with the standards of the time), and that the men who went out sledging were capable of the task.

There are many personal qualities required in anyone wishing to mount such a huge expedition. Qualities such as self-confidence, determination, leadership, organisational ability, and a healthy degree of ambition are certainly key amongst them. How much ambition is too much? At what point does the necessary degree of ambition, tip over into being "overweening"? That is very much a matter of interpretation, and it is a charge most often made by critics in retrospect. If the enterprise is a success, then the leader is usually lavished with praise, and often hailed as a hero. If it fails, or things go awry, the leader is open to the claim that he or she was clearly far too ambitious to start with, that they had "bitten off far more than they could chew." There are few, if any, leaders of *successful* ventures in any field of endeavour, who suffer that particular criticism.

If Ninnis had not died in the crevasse, and he, Mawson and Mertz had all returned to the Hut, exhausted and hungry, but safe, having reached 350 miles east, would Mawson still have been criticised for being too ambitious in his plans? I very much doubt it. It is only that single, defining event of the expedition, which in turn caused Mertz's death, and Mawson's survival by only the narrowest of margins, that leaves Mawson open to such a charge.

Mawson was certainly not the only man who had ambitions. Ninnis in particular was desperate to follow in his father's footsteps and become a 'polar explorer'. He probably articulated the thoughts of many of the men who signed up for the expedition when he wrote:

> If I come through this show all right, by my next Sunday dinner, I shall have performed my object. The Antarctic Continent will have been desecrated by my flat feet. The 'white ribbon' will glisten on my breast, and I shall, I hope be able to hold up my head among these men whose lives have not been wasted, men who have done something. Once again my famous toast—Polar Explorers. But before then two years must elapse, at the very least, and many and various are the hardships and dangers which I must undergo. But it will be the life of a man, not the poodlefacking existence of a nincompoop. All the same I only hope I shall come up to scratch, and not fall far short of the other fellows.[61]

Did Mawson's ambitious program itself therefore cause the deaths of Ninnis and Mertz? I fail to see exactly how. Nor does Day specifically state how he sees Mawson's "overweening ambition" directly causing the deaths of his companions. Therefore it is likely that he is suggesting one of two things. Either that the planned Far Eastern sledge journey of approximately 300 to 400 miles each way, was beyond Mawson's ability, or, he is following Madigan's criticism that Mawson was deliberately travelling in an area where most crevassing was likely to be found, which directly caused the death of Ninnis, and as a consequence, the death of Mertz.

Mawson (with David and MacKay) had completed a journey of 1260 miles by man-hauling, with no support, on the BAE in 1907/8. In light of this experience, his proposed Far Eastern sledge journey of approximately 700 to 800 miles return using dog teams would hardly seem to be an over-reach, or evidence in itself of Mawson's "overweening ambition".

Mawson's Far Eastern sledging journeys on the AAE started on 10 November 1912, and all parties were instructed to return to the Huts by 15 January 1913, a total of up to 67 days "on the trail". The crevasse fall that killed Ninnis occurred on 1 December 1912, (day 35 of the journey). Mawson planned to return via a more inland track, which promised faster travel due to reduced delays crossing the glaciers, and the load to be pulled would be ever decreasing. With this in mind, there is no evidence that Mawson had forced the party to 'press on' significantly beyond a safe turn around date. If that had been the case, it could be considered to be an indication that Mawson was potentially sacrificing the lives of his companions for the sake of his own excessive ambition to reach his goal. In direct comparison, Madigan, leading the coastal surveying journey turned around on 19 December 1912, and Bage leading the Magnetic Pole group turned for home on 21 December 1912. Mawson's turnaround was forced by the tragic circumstances on 15 December 1912, but there is no evidence that he intended to proceed outbound for longer

than was safe, or for longer than either of the other two main parties.
Mawson's stated objective for the sledge journey was:

> to push out rapidly overland to the southward of Madigan's party,
> mapping more distant sections of the coast-line beyond the limit to which
> the latter party would be likely to reach.[62]

Mawson's journey did cross many heavily crevassed areas, and may have been closer to the coast, and therefore closer to Madigan's party, than he intended. However, every time he realised that he was too close to the coast he turned further inland to correct that situation.

We must remember that this was exploration in its purest form. No-one had been there before, the coast had not been properly sighted or charted, either by any previous expedition, or from the ship on this one. The precise contours of the coast were therefore completely unknown. How could Mawson be expected to know where the coast was once he was out of sight of it, and maintain a suitable distance inland? All he could do was guess, and adjust his track inland when he realised that he was getting too close to the coast again. The furthest east point that Mawson reached on his journey was in fact 113 miles south of the latitude of the Huts. In Mawson's 300 mile journey to the east, the coast tended more than one mile *south* for every three miles *east*.

Crevasses can be present just about everywhere there is ice, but it is true that some areas are worse than others. The more inland return route that Mawson took was also crevassed, and even Bage on the South Magnetic Pole journey, reported crevasses on 3 and 4 December 2012, in an area at least 60 miles further inland than Mawson's outbound track.[63] It would not have mattered if Mawson's outbound route had been further to the south, that area was not free of the dangers of crevasses either. Madigan's charge that Mawson was to blame for the death of Ninnis, and as a consequence, the death of Mertz, specifically because the area they were in was more dangerous than any other area due to crevasses, is not sufficiently proven in my opinion.

Day's third accusation is that Mawson's 'poor decision making' caused the deaths of his companions.

This statement relates to the division of stores between the two sledges. Day writes:

> Although Mawson would never admit it, his earlier division of the food
> and fuel between the two sledges was the cause of the dire predicament
> that now confronted them.

This statement appears to be a contradiction of his more detailed examination of this sledge reorganisation just a few pages earlier, where he indicates that Mawson couldn't afford to lose either sledge.[64]

In my opinion Day's earlier summary is the more correct one. Amongst survivalist and bushcraft circles there is a truism known as the "Rule of

Threes". Simply stated, this is that humans can survive extreme environments for three minutes without air, three hours without shelter, three days without water, and three weeks without food.[65] While this is, of course, a massive over-generalisation with numerous exceptions possible, it does adequately reflect the hierarchy of needs in an extreme environment such as Antarctica. Air is clearly not an issue in Antarctica unless you are trapped in a snow cave or an avalanche, but shelter, water and food are significant, and in that order. In Antarctica the biggest threat to survival is exposure, then dehydration, and only lastly, starvation.

An examination of the equipment on each sledge, as detailed by Mawson, shows what equipment was available to meet each of the basic needs. Please note that I am including sleeping bags under the category of requirements for shelter. The expeditioners' outer clothing in this era was not sufficient to keep them warm when they were not on the trail. The tent alone, or an ice shelter, would not have provided sufficient "shelter" against the cold to allow them to sleep in this environment.

Need	Sledge 1 - Mawson	Sledge 2 - Ninnis
Shelter	Spare tent cover	Proper tent with poles
	Sleeping bags	and floor
Water	Primus stove	
	Nansen cooker	
	Fuel	
Food	1.5 weeks food for 2 men (reported)	3.5 weeks food for 3 men (estimated)
Power	6 dogs in poor condition No dog food	6 dogs in average condition All dog food
Navigation	Theodolite	
Other	Private bags	Most tools
	Rifle	Cups and spoons
		Mertz's Burberry trousers and helmet
		Mast and sail for sledge

The division of equipment and food between the sledges appears to have been made primarily on the basis of weight balance or convenience alone, and not on the basis of ensuring any degree of safety or redundancy in the event of the loss of either sledge.

If this was a fatal flaw, then it was a flaw evident in every expedition to Antarctica at that time, with the possible exceptions of Amundsen's South Pole expedition, and the early stages of Scott's last expedition. Every party that had only a single sledge could not have recovered from its loss, and in multi-sledge parties, any party that only had one tent and one stove, was potentially in the same position. The addition of the extra weight required to provide redundancy for critical equipment almost always precluded against its carriage in the minds of the early explorers, since it would significantly limit the amount of exploring they could expect to achieve.

Aside from the tragedy of losing Ninnis, in fact, I believe that Mawson's party was in a substantially better situation having lost the second sledge than they would have been had they lost Mawson's lead sledge.

They had a tent cover and the means to contrive alternative supports for it. They had sleeping bags that enabled them to conserve warmth when resting. They had the stove, the cooker and fuel to provide both sufficient water and warm food; and they had the means to navigate their way back to the Hut. Food, for both themselves and the dogs, was the only essential thing they were critically short of.

The alternate situation would have seen them with a good tent, but no sleeping bags; not able to sleep due to the cold; eating cold food; and without any means to produce water other than by melting snow in their mouths – a method that not only fails to produce *enough* water, but also significantly lowers core body temperature at the same time, and thereby exacerbates the effects of cold exposure.

Their only chance in those circumstances would have been to head for the coast so they could find their way back to base; and there existed the possibility of either meeting Madigan's party, or signalling the ship. If they made it to the coast, they would then have had to try to catch and kill penguins or seals (without a gun) to render blubber to burn; and contrive some sort of stove, so they could melt ice to get enough water. I suggest that if the lead sledge had been lost, both survivors could possibly have been dead within days, rather than weeks, especially if they failed to reach the coast before they died of exposure or dehydration. There are amazing tales of survival against the odds in the Antarctic and elsewhere, and one should never say "impossible", but perhaps, an extremely remote chance of survival for anyone had only the resources of the second sledge been available.

Mawson stated that the sledges were packed with the view that the most critical equipment was on the second sledge, believing that if an accident were to occur, the first sledge would be the most likely to suffer.[66] I believe Mawson is wrong in this statement. Since there was a spare tent cover on the first sledge, in my opinion the next most critical equipment was the stove, the fuel and the sleeping bags. None of those items were on the sledge that Mawson claimed held the most important equipment. Importantly, the outbound journey had demonstrated that both sledges were almost equally subject to crevasse falls, as had happened to the rear sledge on 22 and 23 November 1912.[67]

Even in the 21st century, travel in Antarctica is dangerous. Small parties are still extremely vulnerable if critical equipment is lost or damaged. This has not changed at all since Mawson's days, despite the availability of options for rescue. Castrission and Jones in their 2012 *Crossing the Ice* unsupported return journey to the South Pole paid great attention to safety by having backup equipment, or the means to repair all items and equipment that they considered critical. For example, their equipment list included no fewer than three stoves, but still only one tent. They also had the ability to call for an air evacuation at any time (and multiple means to make the call). Yet they also accepted that if a crisis arose in a period of bad weather, the rescue plane might not be able to land in time to save them, and they could easily have died as a result.[68]

The only way to ensure sufficient backup for most eventualities in Antarctica is to travel in larger parties, such as Amundsen did. I would suggest at least three tents to allow sufficient room to combine one tent party into the other two in the event of the loss of the tent or stove, and sufficient rations to not starve anyone – a party of six to nine people. Had Mawson applied this standard, it would have reduced the number of significant sledging journeys possible from his Winter Quarters from three down to one. This would have had a dramatic impact on the quantum of territory that the expedition could potentially explore.

During my research I was surprised to discover that during the 17 Antarctic expeditions of the Heroic Era, which resulted in the deaths of 19 expeditioners, Ninnis was the only one who was killed in a crevasse.[69] This was despite innumerable reported falls into crevasses and near-misses. Experience had certainly shown Mawson, Ninnis and Mertz the dangers of crevasses before the tragedy occurred, but to that date, the only fatality in a crevasse was one of the ponies on Shackleton's furthest south journey. They may have thought that the dangers of crevasses were reasonably well understood, and, for the most part, manageable.

Day also writes of Madigan being disgusted by the way Mawson spoke about the deaths of Ninnis and Mertz:

> *which suggests that Mawson tried to shift the responsibility for the two deaths onto the men themselves – that they had knowingly embarked on a dangerous expedition and had been the authors of their own misfortune. If he made such comments to Madigan and the others, it is no wonder that Madigan was angry.*[70]

This seems like a strange comment for Day to make. We do not know exactly what it was that Mawson said that made Madigan so angry, because Madigan does not say. However, I cannot imagine it was this.

Firstly, it is a statement of the obvious. Every single member of the expedition had knowingly embarked on a dangerous venture into unknown territory. It is ridiculous to suggest that they were unaware of the potential risks. Many of the men, including Mawson, and Madigan, wrote final farewell letters to loved ones before they went out sledging, which shows that that they were acutely aware of the risks involved.

[37]

Ninnis's diary particularly reveals a complete understanding that he was undertaking a dangerous expedition and may die as a result. Many of his diary entries, some even before he left home, are heart-breakingly prescient:

> My departure is always in my mind now. 'The last time' of doing things, visiting places, or seeing people is begin[ning] to obtrude itself in its usual grisly style, and glad and proud as I am to be going with this Expedition, I cannot say I look forward to the actual moment when the Aurora casts off; and there is no getting over the fact that there is more than a chance of never returning home.[71]

And, just prior to departing on the Far Eastern sledge journey:

> It is very pleasant to be packing to return home, and one wonders, or rather anticipates with joy, the unpacking at home, free at last from this cursed wind but we all have at the back of our minds, a bit of speculation as to whether we ourselves shall ever unpack the gear we are now stowing, or whether it will only be forwarded to our homes when the expedition, minus members, returns. It will be interesting to see what the next two months will produce. Never before will any parties have attempted to sledge in weather in any way approaching that which must be our daily lot.[72]

Secondly, Ninnis was killed, and the sledge was lost, in a crevasse fall. Whether that was an avoidable situation or not, just about every single member of the expedition who had ventured away from the Huts, including Madigan himself, had the experience of encountering crevasses, and minor falls into them, so they all understood intimately just how very easily such an incident could happen.

And lastly, the immediate cause of Mertz's death was illness of some kind, whatever the cause, and no-one except Day has tried to lay the blame for that on Mawson.

If leaders bear the ultimate responsibility for deaths under their command, irrespective of the individual circumstances of those deaths, then looking at the three other major expedition leaders of the "Heroic Era" Scott was responsible for by far the greatest number of deaths - eight across his two expeditions - including his own death and that of the other four members of his South Pole Party. Shackleton was responsible for more deaths than Mawson. It is often said that Shackleton never lost a man. However, most people forget about the Ross Sea Party of the TAE. Although this group was not under Shackleton's personal command, they were part of his expedition, and three men died trying to meet their commitment to provide support for Shackleton's crossing of Antarctica under almost impossible circumstances. Amundsen was the only one to return from Antarctica with all of his men.

[38]

So was Mawson ultimately responsible for the deaths of Ninnis and Mertz?

As the leader he was responsible for devising and equipping the expedition, and for putting himself, and his men, in a situation that could potentially lead to their deaths. However, no-one forced Ninnis and Mertz or anyone else to apply to go on the Expedition. They were all aware that an Antarctic expedition was a dangerous enterprise, and were willing participants in it.

Risk existed in all aspects of exploration at that time, and still does today. Gene Kranz, former Deputy Director of NASA Mission Operations, has put it this way:

> Risk is the price of progress. It is the price explorers and their guides must pay to chart new paths. It is the price of discovery.[73]

Mawson and his team thought they had worked out a system for crossing crevasses with relative safety and had done so hundreds of times. However, the very nature of crevasses renders any such system imperfect. Additionally, familiarity breeds complacency, in this case with tragic results. Despite the presence of Mertz on the expedition, and some attempts by most members to learn to use skis, Mawson apparently remained unconvinced of their value in the type of landscape they found themselves in, and so Mertz was the only member of the sledging journeys who took or used skis. It is entirely possible – as many have suggested – that Ninnis may not have died if he had been on skis, using snowshoes, or riding on the sledge. It is equally possible that the bridge over the crevasse had been fatally weakened by the passage of Mawson and the first sledge, and nothing would have saved him. We can never know. Even Amundsen, the generally acknowledged master of polar travel using dogs and skis, had some very close shaves with crevasses on his South Pole expedition.[74] They are an ever present danger in Antarctica. Even modern mechanised transport is still not safe from crevasse falls and deaths.[75]

In Mawson's choice of equipment, he was a product of his times and experience. He learnt mainly from Scott and Shackleton. Neither of his mentors made great use of skis or snowshoes for Antarctic travel, but neither lost a man in a crevasse, despite travelling extensively on glaciers where crevasses are common.

Unlike Scott and Shackleton, Mawson had appreciated the value of dogs and had made reasonably good use of them, definitely better use than was made by Scott on the NAE, although Day is correct in stating that the food Mawson provided for them seemed inadequate.[76] This is the one area where Ninnis was also highly critical of Mawson.[77] In many ways Mawson showed a considerable ability to look beyond the methods of his mentors, to learn from others outside the British tradition, and to innovate, but that did not extend to a full appreciation of the benefits of skis.

We cannot use 20/20 hindsight, and the knowledge and standards of safety we have today, to sit in judgement on an expedition that took place more than 100 years ago. Rather, Mawson should be judged in light of the knowledge and standards of his time, and that is not so easy to do. We forget that our attitudes are not remotely similar to the attitudes common at that time, and people who are not intimately connected with safety management also do not fully appreciate that modern safety practices have evolved through a process of incremental change, and mostly as a result of learning gained the very hardest way – through a litany of near-misses, accidents, deaths, and disasters. This process is continuous, and ongoing.

For example, we find it appalling now that the *Titanic* carried insufficient lifeboats to accommodate all of the people on board. But we forget that the *Titanic's* lifeboat capacity exceeded the required standards of the time.[78] Were the owners and designers of the *Titanic* criminally negligent? Enquiries on both sides of the Atlantic found them not to be so. However, that disaster was the impetus for the implementation of the International Convention for the Safety of Life at Sea, still in force today. There is still room for improvement however, and the recent *Costa Concordia* disaster has already led to further enhancements in safety procedures on cruise ships. We simply cannot expect that things that may seem obvious to us now with the full benefits of hindsight, such as the advantages of skis for Antarctic travel, or the need for enough lifeboats to accommodate all of the passengers and crew on a cruise ship, were at all obvious to the people of the past.

The judgement of Mawson's contemporary explorer, and the man with the greatest Antarctic experience at that time, is relevant in this context. Contemporary newspaper reports quote Shackleton as saying:

> *A portion of the press in speaking of the Mawson Antarctic Expedition calls it the Mawson Antarctic Tragedy. Undoubtedly the deaths of Lieutenant Ninnis and Dr Mertz are sad, but they were the outcome of accidents which come in the ordinary course of all Polar exploration. Apart from these two accidents, the expedition seems to have been a particularly brilliant one.*[79]

7

Murder by Mutual Starvation?

Mawson put them both on what he called 'extremely low rations' in the hope that Mertz would die before he did and that Mawson might then survive on the remaining rations.[80]

This is Day's most controversial new idea, and the suggestion that does most damage to Mawson's reputation. It is a suggestion that could never have been published while Mawson was alive if the author wanted to avoid a suit for defamation. There have been previous intimations that Mawson may have cannibalised Mertz's dead body, but Day is now suggesting actions that would be tantamount to deliberate murder, a far worse crime.[81]

What an insanely risky scenario this would be for anyone to contemplate. It reads more like the plot of a very bad detective novel; the only elements missing are the poison in your companion's food and the antidote in your own.

Mertz was younger than Mawson by two years, a ski-champion and mountaineer, presumably a very fit man, possibly fitter even than Mawson himself. Mawson had undergone severely restricted rations previously on the BAE. How was he to know that his own constitution had not suffered significant and possibly lasting damage as a result? Perhaps he may have been *more* likely to die first, not *less* likely. This idea makes so little sense that I cannot believe it would be contemplated by anyone. More importantly, there is simply no evidence that Mawson ever thought that way.

The only 'evidence' that Day cites for this theory is that Mawson changed his approach to rationing after Mertz's death. He started to eat more food, and to eat on days he could not travel, when previously the two of them had eaten little, if anything, if they could not travel.[82] Day's statement that this supports his theory seems entirely illogical. Of course Mawson changed his rationing after Mertz had died. It does not matter how much food there was, or how long the food had been budgeted to last for, it had been budgeted for *two* people. Eating more after Mertz had died, even if travel was not possible, was an entirely sensible response to the significant change in circumstances, and a very long way from being evidence of a deliberate scheme to starve his companion to death.

What does Day expect Mawson to have done – maintain the previous level of rations and thereby double the number of days that the food would last? This would be pointless. Instead Mawson reassessed his position thoughtfully following Mertz's death. With Mertz's illness and death he had only covered two miles since 4 January 1913. Mertz died on 8 January, and Mawson remained camped until 11 January, burying Mertz's body, and reorganising his equipment. Just cutting down the sledge must have taken a significant amount of time and physical effort. It hardly seems surprising that on 9 January Mawson wanted to "have more to eat today in the hope that it will give me strength for the future."[83] He would barely have had the strength to even move if he had hardly eaten in five days.

The most absurd part of Day's entire argument is that had an 'evil' Mawson decided that there was only enough food for one person to survive, why would he let Mertz have any? There were other far easier ways to kill Mertz if that was what Mawson had concluded was necessary, and more importantly, methods that did not include half killing himself in the process. They had a rifle. They were surrounded by crevasses. Mawson could have done away with Mertz very easily, or vice versa, and no one would ever have known. Fortunately, we do know that Mawson did not do any of that, because Mertz's diary survives, carefully preserved by Mawson, and carried back to the Huts.

While I believe that Day's suggestion is both illogical and extremely unlikely, for his idea to have any validity the rations would have to be cut to an unreasonably low level. To analyse this, we need to understand how much food was available, and how it was rationed, and how long it was budgeted to last for.

Unfortunately, we cannot be entirely certain how the food was rationed. Mawson mentions keeping food and distance logs, but these have not been published.[84] Mawson also reported adjusting the rations up and down according to the distance travelled. This makes any attempt at analysing the rationing almost impossible.[85] There are also numerous references made to cooking dog meat. We do not know, because Mawson does not explain, whether all the dog meat was cooked straight away as each dog was killed, whether it was fully cooked or only part cooked, or whether some of it was allowed to freeze while raw and was carried on the sledge.[86] We do not know the details, and probably never will.

The only thing that is known, from all accounts, is that after the loss of Ninnis and his sledge in the crevasse, there was "one and a half weeks of food" plus six dogs, definitely not in the most prime condition.[87]

To try to make some sense of how Mawson may have budgeted the food available, I have created some basic data modelling of the situation. The critical decision to be made is: how long did Mawson and Mertz need to make the available food last?

The outward journey, under canine power took 34 days. Taking that number of days as a starting point, it is possible to consider what allowances should be made for the changed circumstances, to enable an estimation of the time required for the return journey. The following factors are significant:

Fewer dogs, dogs in poor condition with little or no food, and reducing number of dogs as they are killed one by one for food. Eventually, manhauling being the only motive power. Add 30%.

Weather delays - there were weather days included in the outbound journey. Add a further 5% for contingency.

Reduced distances covered due to declining strength caused by starvation. Add 20%.

Sledge much lighter each day as food and fuel consumed. Deduct 5%.

Less terrain delays on inland route chosen, however the distance is longer. Deduct 5%.

These adjustments are my own estimations, others may have different ideas. The result of the above estimate, adding the various factors, would be that the return journey might take up to 45% longer than the outward journey, so a total of 50 days. Therefore the food should be rationed to last for this amount of time to cover for most contingencies. This would mean average distance each day would need to be just 6 miles, a distance that would appear to be quite achievable. Average daily distance covered on the outbound journey was 8.8 miles.

In this position, the most sensible thing to do is to cut your rations immediately, and by as much as you need to, in order to make them last as long as you expect the journey *might possibly take*. If you travel faster than expected, you can always *increase* the rations later in the journey when you think it safe to do so. Unfortunately, you cannot recover your position if you budget too generously to start with, and then travel more slowly than expected. In that situation you simply run out of food completely.

How long would the available food last?

Available food on Mawson's sledge: 10.5 days full ration for 2 men		
Percentage of standard ration	Number of days for 2 men	Food Lasts Until
50% - Half	21	3 Jan
33% - One third	31.5	14 Jan
25% - One quarter	42	24 Jan
20% - One fifth	52.5	4 Feb
17% - One sixth	63	14 Feb

How much food is that per day?

Rations in ounces	Full	1/2	1/3	1/4	1/5	1/6
		50%	33%	25%	20%	17%
Biscuit	12	6.00	3.96	3.00	2.40	1.99
Pemmican	8	4.00	2.64	2.00	1.60	1.33
Butter	2	1.00	0.66	0.50	0.40	0.33
Chocolate	2	1.00	0.66	0.50	0.40	0.33
Milk (glaxo)	5	2.50	1.65	1.25	1.00	0.83
Sugar	4	2.00	1.32	1.00	0.80	0.66
Cocoa	1	0.50	0.33	0.25	0.20	0.17
Tea	0.25	0.13	0.08	0.06	0.05	0.04
Total ounces	34.25	17.13	11.30	8.56	6.85	5.69

To make the food last for 50 days, rations would need to be cut to between one quarter and one fifth of the standard amount, approximately 7.2 ounces per day for each man, plus a portion of the dog meat.

To compare my calculated estimates with the actual events, we need examine the very little information we have about how much food was actually being consumed. Mawson makes only a few specific mentions of this.

Firstly, that the daily ration Mawson reports on 17 December 1912 was about 6 ounces of ordinary food and about 8 to10 ounces of dog meat.[88]   In total, this is less than half the amount of food provided by the standard sledging ration. The 6 ounces of ordinary food is slightly less than my estimate above, so it is entirely possible that Mawson was either trying to make the food last for longer than 50 days, or, he was using less of the standard ration and more of the dog meat during the early part of the return journey. It would certainly make sense to eat mostly dog meat on the days that the dogs were killed and the meat was fresh – that way less of the meat would have to be carried on the sledge.

The second definite reference we have from Mawson is that he mentions starting a new food bag on 4 January.[89] Since ration bags were packed for a full week it would appear that the half week's food, 3.5 days worth, had been stretched out to last for 21 days from 14 December 1912 to 4 January 1913.

To make the part bag of food last for 21 days, it had to have been allocated at about one sixth of standard rations or 5.69 oz. This is consistent with Mawson's previous report of 6 oz daily.

3.5 days of rations for 2 people
50% rations - 7 days
33% rations - 10.5 days
25% rations - 14 days
20% rations - 17.5 days
17% rations - 21 days

The final references that we have are that there was approximately 4 or 5 pounds of food left on 26 January 1912, so somewhere between 64 and 80 ounces, and on 28 January 1912 when the rescue party's cache was found, all that Mawson had left was "twenty small chips of cooked dog meat in addition to half a pound of raisins and a few ounces of chocolate."[90]

The full ration for two men for one week would have weighed just under 30 lbs – 29.97 lbs or 479.5 oz to be precise. The full bag was started on 4 January. So using Mawson's earlier reported estimates of 6 oz of ration foods per man per day while Mertz was alive, and assuming that Mawson ate double that amount – 12 oz per day, after Mertz died, then there should have been 203.5 oz (12.7 pounds) left at 26 January. It appears therefore that Mawson was eating more than his previously reported amount of the ration foods, possibly because there was less dog meat available by this time.

In order to finish up with the amounts of food that Mawson reports as remaining, and assuming equal division of rations while Mertz was alive, then the quantity eaten from this full bag would need to be approximately 9 oz of sledging rations per man per day for the two of them, then 18 oz per day for Mawson alone, from 4 January to 26 January. With what he reports as having left on 28th January, it also seems that Mawson had not evenly divided and consumed all the ration foods in balanced daily amounts. For example, he had no pemmican or biscuit left.

Returning to my own notional food budget, in order to make this bag of food started on 4 January last until 1 February – the remaining 24 days of my budgeted total of 50 days of return travel, then the amount available per day under this scenario is 16.5 ounces.

Mawson would have had difficulty dividing the food into smaller and smaller portions, and accurately measuring portions with limited equipment. There is also the unknown factor of how much dog meat there was, and what food was actually being consumed each day. Considering these factors, I believe that the correlation between the limited firm evidence from Mawson's published diary, and my estimates, is reasonably close – within 1.5 ounces per day, with Mawson's actual consumption being higher than my notional 50 day budget.

Therefore it seems there is no evidence that Mawson cut the food rations significantly below a level that was consistent with allowing food for two men for enough time needed to ensure reaching the Huts.

There is another important factor to be considered in analysing Day's controversial suggestion. Where does Mertz fit in? For Day's idea to have any validity, Mawson would have to have been the sole decision maker and sole controller of rations, and have forced Mertz to submit to his will. In the extraordinary circumstances in which they found themselves, it is equally likely that the formal leadership position was abandoned, or at least relaxed, and that Mawson and Mertz made critical decisions about what course of action to take, and how to ration their extremely limited food, together as equals. In this case, Mertz would have been a willing and active participant in the rationing regime. Mawson states in his diary, "We divide up stores..," and "we decide to camp in hope that it will be better light by noon...".[91] Later, when Mertz was ill "eventually we decided to rest today..."[92] These entries indicate at least the possibility that such important decisions were made by mutual consent, and not by Mawson alone.

Given Mawson's extremely debilitated condition at the end of his journey, when he had been able to eat rations budgeted for two people for a significant portion of it, it would seem very unlikely that both Mawson and Mertz could have survived to reach Winter Quarters on the amount of food they had available. However, it is impossible to factor in how much of an effect the illness they were both suffering, whatever its cause, might have had on the distances they were able to cover each day. The situation could well have been different if they were *only* suffering from reduced rations.

8

What Really Killed Mertz?

Day presents a new theory to explain Mertz's rapid physical decline and death – protein poisoning.[93] This is a condition caused by eating meat with virtually no fat content, little or no fat from other sources, and no carbohydrate. The condition is also known as "rabbit starvation."[94] In the Notes section of his book, Day unequivocally dismisses other theories suggesting Vitamin A poisoning or simple starvation – "Both claims are wrong"[95] – but he is not so completely dismissive of these theories, and also contradicts himself, in the text of the book.

> Then again, feeling 'off colour' might have been due to malnutrition, brought on by the starvation rations that Mawson was imposing on them. Or it might have been due to the vitamin A from dog livers, or the consumption of a diet composed almost totally of lean meat. Most likely the deterioration in their condition was caused by a combination of all these factors.

Later, referring to protein[96] poisoning, he states:

> It is almost certain that the latter condition was principally responsible for Mertz's steady decline.[97]

Mawson states that the dog meat contained virtually no fat, so it is possible that a preponderance of high protein and low fat meat may have been a contributing factor in the declining condition of both men, particularly when it seems likely that during the period that Mertz remained alive there was a greater proportion of dog meat being consumed.[98] However they were not consuming the dog meat at the exclusion of all other food, and Mawson reports in *The Home Of The Blizzard* that they were eating about six ounces of normal foods daily, and that occasionally at least, they were mixing dog meat into pemmican.[99] Since the normal rations consisted substantially of high fat pemmican, butter, and biscuit, we cannot say that their diet was completely lacking in either fat or carbohydrate at any time.

The vitamin A poisoning theory put forward by the qualified medical professionals should not be dismissed so easily.[100] Vitamins had not been discovered at the time of these events, and Mawson did not have the knowledge to suspect any danger in eating the dog livers. He reported enjoying eating the liver because it was easier to chew.[101] Since this was regarded as a relatively prime cut, and more palatable to the men, I believe it unlikely that much, if any, of the liver would have been fed to the remaining dogs. Therefore a substantial amount of it would have been consumed by both Mawson and Mertz, and was likely to have contained a significant overdose of vitamin A. In support of his theory Day has proposed that the vitamin A content of the livers of semi-starved dogs was likely to be lower than usual, because the livers would be smaller, however he gives no evidence or source to support this suggestion.[102]

Interestingly, in putting forward his new theory, Day ignores perhaps the best evidence we are ever likely to get on the subject, which is that provided by Tim Jarvis's re-creation of Mawson's trek in 2007. Although it was not possible for Jarvis to exactly reproduce the conditions Mawson endured, this expedition is the closest anyone is likely to come to doing so without actually killing anyone. Dogs are no longer permitted in Antarctica, and dog meat, especially dog liver, was not used in the re-creation. Instead, extremely lean kangaroo jerky was substituted, so it can be presumed that the fat content of the meat Jarvis ate was similarly low. The clothing and equipment available to Mawson was re-created as closely as possible. Neither Jarvis nor Stoukalo (who played the part of Mertz) suffered any of the symptoms that Mawson and Mertz reported experiencing, such as chronic stomach pain, skin loss or hair loss. They lost a considerable amount of weight and suffered from the normal symptoms consistent with starvation and cold exposure. Jarvis appears convinced that the dog livers Mawson and Mertz ate played a significant part in Mertz's death and Mawson's physical decline.

> The difference leads almost without doubt to the fact that the dog livers and the Vitamin A within them must have been a major factor in Mertz's death, but perhaps not the only one.[103]

None of the theories of what caused the illness explain why Mertz died first, and in a matter of just 26 days. There are four significant factors to differentiate between Mawson and Mertz.

Firstly, Mertz is likely to have suffered much worse from cold exposure due to the loss of his burberry trousers and helmet in the crevasse. He was able to substitute only a pair of thick woollen under-trousers, and they are unlikely to have been as effective as the burberry gabardine cloth.

Secondly, Mertz may possibly have started the return journey from the crevasse in a position of greater calorie deficit than Mawson. The sledging rations, even at full quantity, probably did not provide sufficient calories for the energy they were expending, doing hard physical work in extremely cold conditions. Normally sledgers report being unable to eat the full ration in the early days of a journey, and then gradually becoming more and more voracious as their energy reserves are expended.[104] Mawson states that their usual order of travel was to have someone out front leading, followed by the sledges under the charge of the other two, with himself always on the first sledges (when he was not leading out front), and Mertz and Ninnis rotating management of the rear sledge. When conditions permitted use of skis, Mertz was usually in the lead position. He wrote "on many occasions when the sledges were running easily, two of us were able to ride."[105]   One of those occasions was while Mawson was calculating position at the time that Ninnis and his sledge were tragically lost in the crevasse. At the start of the sledge journey, when several parties were in close proximity for a few days, Madigan reports seeing "old Mawson sitting on a sledge with cap off, yelling and waving like a boy."[106]

If Mawson *had* spent a significant amount of time riding on the sledge when conditions were suitable, and Mertz *was* more frequently in the lead on skis than either Ninnis or Mawson on foot, then it is possible that Mawson had expended significantly less energy over the outbound journey in comparison to Mertz. It is impossible to quantify this, but it might have been one factor contributing to Mertz's more rapid decline.

The two other possible explanations are differing physiology, and psychology, between the two men. Individuals differ significantly in their responses to food, starvation, diseases and toxins, with some being more severely affected than others, and at differing rates;[107] however detailed examination of this point would be the domain of medical professionals.

The effects of an individual's psychology on their chances of survival are well documented. Mental attitude and the will to live play a part in many cases of survival against the odds.[108] Perhaps Mawson was simply better equipped mentally to deal with the situation than Mertz, and had a greater motivation for survival.

9

Finding the Way Home?

Day makes much of Madigan's accusation that Mawson was not a competent navigator, and repeatedly refers to Mawson's apparent confusion about position during his Far Eastern sledge journey:

> *In fact, Mawson had been uncertain about his position from the beginning of the journey.*[109]

On their first preliminary sledge journey, Mawson and Madigan had argued about the correct course to follow. Later when Madigan was "practising" taking sights and working out the position, he accused Mawson of not knowing how to do the calculations.[110] Mawson also reports that Webb expressed doubt about his (Mawson's) ability in this regard, and about Madigan's "astronomical work".[111]

These days, just about everyone has a GPS device in their pocket, so it is very easy to forget how difficult it was to work out precisely where you are on the surface of the Earth without one. Most people have little, if any, understanding of how it was done. It required taking sights of the sun or stars using a sextant or theodolite, use of reference tables, and complex mathematical calculations (without benefit of an electronic calculator) to work out the latitude and longitude.

Frequent excision notations in the published version of Mawson's diaries indicate that navigation calculations are there in the original manuscript, but have been edited out since they are of no interest to the general reader. Surely anyone skilled in this field would be able to assess whether these calculations, and the methods used, were correct or not. However, I am not aware of this having ever been done. Did Mawson ever present his data to the Royal Geographical Society for verification as explorers frequently did at that time?

Madigan does mention that Mawson asked him to help check the positions, and that Mawson subsequently worked with Bage to "find out where he went while sledging, as none of his observations agree with the sledgemeter".[112] The comment about the sledgemeter is not at all surprising, since its accuracy was in doubt from the start of the journey when it was damaged, and it required repair several times. Madigan should not have found this remarkable either, since his own sledgemeter was also a constant source of problems and also probably highly inaccurate.[113]

To evaluate Day's assertion, we need to try to assess whether Mawson was a competent navigator or not.

Edgeworth David is reported to have praised Mawson for his "extraordinary skill as a navigator."[114]   David was not only a respected professor, but also a veteran of the single longest unsupported sledge journey to that date on the South Magnetic Pole journey on Shackleton's Nimrod expedition in 1909 with Mawson.   David had observed Mawson as a navigator in action.   David's narrative in *Heart of the Antarctic* tells us that Mawson did the vast majority of the theodolite observations, position observations and calculations, and magnetic observations on that journey.[115]

In contrast Cecil Madigan had been on no major expedition, and exactly what experience he may have had in navigation is not known.   However, he makes a couple of interesting references to that experience, or lack thereof.   On 23 November 1911, prior to departure he says:

> *I begin to repent of my little-deserved reputation for understanding the theodolite and position observations, as I am to be the last to get practice.*[116]

Later, after mentioning his appointment as Navigator on 29 December, he refers to studying navigation on the voyage south, and working on navigation problems.[117]   Madigan was "practicing" taking navigational observations when he came to the conclusion that Mawson did not know what he was doing.[118] It is entirely possible that Madigan may not have known how to do these calculations sufficiently well himself.   Did he have any right to criticise Mawson in this regard?   We cannot really say with any certainty, but it is possible that Madigan had less knowledge, and almost certainly less experience, than Mawson.

David Day writes as if he has an understanding of the issues involved in the practice of dead reckoning navigation, particularly in the circumstances Mawson encountered.   However he does not seem to understand that the inevitable result of dead reckoning, is that the navigator must, by very definition of the process, be 'uncertain of their position' for a very substantial amount of the time.   When travelling in uncharted territory, without significant landmarks, the navigator using dead reckoning is repeatedly in a situation of moving from a known position (after taking sights and calculating position), to an estimated position, based on the measurement of distance and direction travelled, until it is possible to again verify that position by means of taking more sights, and calculating the actual latitude and longitude again.

To be utterly pedantic, the navigator does not 'know' their position from the moment they lose sight of either the location of the last position observation, or of a known and charted landmark.   From that moment on, their 'position' is always only an estimate.   When travelling in unexplored territory it is quite simply impossible to 'know' your position accurately at all times without the use of modern devices such as GPS.

In practice, dead reckoning on land works like this:
1. Take sights and determine position.
2. Work out direction of travel needed to reach your destination, allowing for drift factors. Drift caused by strong wind is less significant on land than on water or in the air, but is still significant.
3. Proceed in that direction, preferably using compass guidance or a visual reference point.
4. Repeat steps 1 to 3 at least daily until destination reached.

However, simply walking in the right direction is not necessarily easy without a visual reference such as a landscape feature to aim for; or another reliable means to determine the direction of travel, such as a functioning compass. It is not easy to ensure you are heading in the right direction if it is necessary to zigzag to avoid obstacles and then try to resume the correct track when there is no reference point to aim for. Humans are not capable of walking a straight line without external references.[119] It is really quite a difficult task in Antarctica where there may be few sufficiently distinctive visible landmarks; magnetic compasses do not work very well due to the proximity of the Magnetic Pole; and the sun compass is useless if the sun is obscured. Most Antarctic expeditions report judging direction of travel by the angle at which they were crossing sastrugi (wind driven snow waves). This seems to work well enough in locations where there are sastrugi.

In a good day's travel on foot of 15 miles, an error of just four degrees in the track made good will result in approximately one mile lateral difference from the planned route; and for every extra four degrees of error, you will be a further mile off track. The problem really escalates when it becomes impossible to take further observations to confirm the new actual position, and redefine the desired heading. The errors start to rapidly compound, and the longer travel continues without being able to take position observations, the worse the situation will get.

Therefore, when Mawson was unable to get a sight, of course he was uncertain of where he was, and he would definitely have had some doubt about what heading he needed to take. If he had experienced conditions where he was frequently forced to divert around obstacles, he could have been in doubt that he had returned to the correct heading, and the distances measured by the sledgemeter, whether accurate or not in terms of actual distance covered, do not reflect the distance made good along the desired track to destination.

Mawson made frequent diary entries along these lines. In doing so, I believe that he was stating the facts inherent in the dead reckoning navigation process. Facts that would be understandable to any navigator, or to any polar traveller familiar with similar conditions. This does not mean that he was either an incompetent navigator, or wandered around lost for the entire journey. Yet this is the mistaken impression the non-expert reader will gain from David Day's very frequently repeated remarks.

The only actual sign of navigational incompetence that I can find in Mawson's published diaries, is that the chronometer stopped because he forgot to wind it. This should not have happened, but it is certainly a small task that could easily be forgotten, and was correctable by means of taking an astronomical observation.

The fact is that at that time, and under the circumstances Mawson was facing, no navigator, no matter how competent, would know exactly where they were and what course they needed to follow at all times. In such situations, dead reckoning navigation is nothing more than educated guesswork.

Notably Day does not mention a statement made by John King Davis, who was renowned for his skill as a navigator, yet he reported on Aurora on 30 January, 1913 "our compass is hopeless and there is no sun, so we do not know what courses we are really making."[120]

The only way to determine the objective truth is for Mawson's observations and calculations to be independently examined. Since Day makes no mention of this having been done and Mawson's ability or lack thereof as a navigator objectively confirmed, I assume that such an exercise has not been carried out.

In Mawson's defence, the best piece of evidence available is the result of his navigation efforts. He found his way back to the Huts across 300 miles of Antarctica with a sledgemeter of dubious accuracy; a theodolite used resting on the cooker box (not on its proper legs, since they were being used to hold up the tent for much of the journey); a chronometer that stopped because he forgot to wind it; a magnetic compass that was unreliable and difficult to use since they were too close to the magnetic pole; and a sun compass that only worked when there was sufficient sun, which was not very often. With all of these problems, plus appalling weather conditions, semi-starvation, and seriously failing health, Mawson walked towards Winter Quarters on almost the exact track he was expected to use, and reached a food drop left by a rescue party that probably helped to save his life.

Was this just unbelievably good luck? Was it divine guidance? Or might Mawson have had at least some skill as a navigator?

10

Jealousy?

The information in McLean's note gave Mawson much to think about. He had been worried that one or more of the other parties might have met with tragedy, which would add to the pall that would be cast over the expedition by the deaths of Ninnis and Mertz. Now he could set his mind at rest on that score. He would also have been reassured by the news that Bickerton's party had only gone 160 miles west, that Bage hadn't reached the South Magnetic Pole, and that Madigan had fallen short of going 300 miles to the east. This left his journey as the longest. Other information from McLean was less reassuring. Mawson learned that Amundsen had reached the South Pole...and that Scott's fate was unknown. Their stories were likely to overshadow the story of Mawson's expedition and his standing as a polar hero, which would affect what he was likely to earn from publishing deals and lecture tours.[121]

How does anyone know what thoughts are running through another's head at any particular time? The only way to really know is if they tell us that it was so. For historical figures, that must be in written form, or reported to someone else, and that second hand account written down or passed on in some way. Even the value of such second hand reports can be questionable, but possibly better than no evidence at all. For Mawson, the only significant evidence of what he was thinking is what he wrote in his diary, and in *The Home Of The Blizzard*.

It is certainly understandable that any leader in Mawson's situation would be concerned for the safety of the others under his command, especially when he, the most experienced member of the group, had come to such grief in his own journey. But reassured that they had not done better than him? This is another of the points that Day repeats numerous times, as if there was some kind of contest going on to determine whose journey was longest, and that Mawson had to win in order to make himself out to be the hero, which is exactly what Day contends he was trying to do.

Mawson's diary entries for the entire sledging journey contain virtually no mention of the other parties at all after the groups separated on 17 November, except to mention that his party did not visit a landmark seen on the coast since they assumed Madigan would. Instead the diaries are full of terrain, weather, distance, navigation, dogs and mentions only of Ninnis and Mertz and his own activities. The only reference to possible concern for other parties is made on 8 January shortly after Mertz's death:

> this awful weather is quite unlooked for and I deeply hope it has not caught any of the party short of food.[122]

This is a remark that shows a spirit of compassion rather than competition. There is no mention whatsoever of any concern for how far the other parties might have travelled or worry that their achievement may outshine his own.

Mawson's published account fleshes out the diary entries considerably, but still makes no mention of any thoughts about comparisons of the distance of his journey to that of the others.

The reference Day gives for this paragraph in his book is Mawson's diary for 29-30 January. These entries refer only to finding the cairn, the food and the note, and directions to Aladdin's Cave. They do not make any mention of the other parties, or of Scott and Amundsen. On the basis of Mawson's writings, this paragraph is revealed as pure speculation from Day. That is not to deny that Mawson may possibly have thought this way, only that there is no evidence of it from his writings if he did.

Since Mawson had planned the longest journey, and was the only one using the dog teams, when all of the others were man-hauling, it is entirely logical that he, and everyone else, would have expected that his team would cover the greatest distance. It would be most surprising if it had not. But all did not go well on his journey, and under the circumstances, it is equally possible that at the end of it Mawson would have been both pleased and grateful that the others had done well, and there may be some decent results to show for their efforts, and for the expedition as a whole. But there is no direct evidence for that thought either.

Day's comments about Amundsen's success, and Scott's probable success, being of concern to Mawson in terms of overshadowing his achievement, and limiting his income potential are interesting. The news can hardly have come as a surprise, since Mawson was well aware that both Amundsen and Scott were on expedition in Antarctica aiming for the South Pole at the same time. He had been aware of Scott's expedition from the commencement of his own planning, since he had been offered a place on it, but had turned Scott down. In fact an article in The Sydney Morning Herald on 30 March 1911 reports him saying in an interview in London that "he was quite sure that Captain Scott could reach the Pole".[123] Mawson makes no reference at all to Scott or Amundsen in the diary entries referenced by Day, or any other entries during his sledging journey.

There is nothing wrong with historians speculating about what someone might have been thinking. Speculation is a legitimate part of modern analysis and interpretation of historical events. However, it is incumbent upon a professional historian to make very clear for the reader what is fact, what is interpretation supported by evidence, and what is the author's own speculation. A professional historian should not give speculation the appearance of fact, and reference it to a source that does not provide evidence for it.

If Mawson makes no mention of competing for distance, where has this idea come from?

Madigan makes some references to his hopes for a long journey. When Mawson announced final arrangements for the sledging parties Madigan says of his own east coast journey "this would be very nice, scientific work, but not *distance*. I imagine he thinks this is better for me."[124] (Italics are as per the printed version.)

Early in the journey on 14 November 2012 Madigan hopes that a distance of 600 miles was possible. Presumably he is talking about return distance here.[125] However, when it came to the crunch, rather than push for stupid distances, Madigan fulfilled Mawson's instructions. He did push outbound for one day beyond what he initially calculated as his turn around date, and was one day late back to the Hut having experienced weather delays on the return. He completed the surveying and magnetic observations requested. There are no further mentions in Madigan's diary for the period of his sledge journey of any desire to compete with or to outdo Mawson's distance.[126]

Day's emphasis on this idea of Mawson being in some kind of competition for distance continues further in his discussion of Bage, Webb and Hurley's Magnetic Pole party. He also states that the men wagered chocolate on which of the sledging teams would go the furthest.[127] This would not be at all surprising, since this bunch of young, mostly Aussie blokes, regularly bet on who could guess closest to the average wind speed every month, and devised their own roulette gaming system. However, neither Mawson, Hunter, Stillwell, or Madigan mention betting on sledging distances in their diaries. I do find it somewhat difficult to believe that even the most inveterate gambler would be willing to wager on men on foot being able to outdistance the dogs. The only person I have found who mentions a wager over distance is Ninnis, who states that he bet Bickerton that the dogs would outdo the air tractor.[128]

The members of these sledging parties were all young, fit, men. It is highly likely that there was a certain amount of competitiveness and rivalry amongst them, whether good-natured or not, but I have not found any trace of it in Mawson's writings.

11

Waiting?

Day is severely critical of Mawson's lengthy delay at Aladdin's cave before proceeding down the icy slope to the Huts. Having reached the cave on the evening of 1 February 1913, he did not leave it until 8 February. The crampons he had made for himself the previous day had fallen apart, and he needed to either find or make more in order to safely proceed down the final ice slope. At that point the blizzard set in, and Mawson was caught.

The lowest wind speed Mawson reports in this time was 35-40 mph on 2 February for about six hours. Day suggests this was "relatively light wind".[129] It may well be relatively light for that part of Antarctica, but the Beaufort scale classifies this wind speed as Force 7 to Force 8, described as "near gale" or "gale". Day considers this to be reasonable conditions for Mawson to walk five and a half miles down an ice slope that descends 2000 feet, which he himself has described as "treacherous" and having a "difficult surface"[130], with no crampons, and the wind at his back, in his severely compromised physical condition.[131]

This is an unreasonable judgement. Such wind could easily knock a man in Mawson's condition off his feet while walking downhill on ice without crampons. Having almost miraculously survived the events so far, why would Mawson risk serious injury or death in the final few miles when he was in a position of safety with plenty of food? How unutterably stupid would it have been for him to have died almost within sight of the Huts.

Had there been no food at Aladdin's cave, Mawson's actions may well have been very different. As it was, can he really be blamed for not taking this last risk? Day has said that Mawson should have proceeded immediately, since he did not know how long the ship would wait. But for all Mawson knew on the evening of 1 February when he reached the cave, the ship could have left already.

Mawson's assessment of the wind on 2 February is independently verified by Davis, whose journal reports the wind at sea as Force 10, "blowing a heavy gale from SE all day. Very heavy drift coming over the ice slope, like smoke."[132] The first opportunity Davis had to get to get the members of the shore party who were leaving Antarctica on board the Aurora, was on the morning of 8 February.

Even the embittered and grieving Madigan supports Mawson's assessment of the conditions, since much fitter men than Mawson were also unable to proceed from the Hut up to the cave, travelling into the wind.

> On February 1st a party was ready to go up to the 5½ mile camp to look around, but the heavy weather which kept the ship in the bay till February 8, prevented them from starting; and Mawson had been up at the Cave from the 1st unable to get down! [133]

Davis had in fact intended to sail on 1 February,[134] and Mawson did not reach Aladdin's cave until the evening of that date. In reality, the windstorm, and Mawson's decision to wait it out in the cave, made no difference whatsoever to the necessity for a relief party to remain. From the moment McLean, Hurley and Hodgeman's land search party turned back, having failed to locate Mawson on 29 January; Mawson had missed his only chance to depart with the ship.

12

Sick?

Day has made some inconsistent statements concerning Mawson's physical condition when he made it back to the huts. First he is "mentally and physically exhausted beyond measure."[135] Then a few pages later;

> If Mawson was in as poor condition as he claimed to have been, it's difficult to know why none of his companions ever provided an independent description of their leader's state.[136]

Having asked that question, with its implication that Mawson may have been exaggerating the effects of his deprivation and illness, just one page later Day states "in fact, it would take him months to recover fully."[137] This latter statement agrees with the evidence as provided by Mawson's diary entries where he reports suffering from the after-effects of his trek until well into July, more than five months after reaching the Huts.[138]

Reviewing Dr McLean's diary opens up the possibility of a different interpretation.[139] As Day states, McLean's diary does not mention Mawson's condition. However, this is his *personal* diary. I believe that it is likely that a doctor would not consider his personal diary to be an appropriate repository for medical notes concerning a man who was not only his patient, but also the expedition leader.

There were only six significant medical events during the expedition that we know about. To my mind 'significant' includes injuries requiring stitches, or treatment under anaesthesia. The various diary writers obviously regarded these events as worthy of recording. They were probably an unusual and dramatic highlight on an otherwise ordinary day.

John Hunter crushed two fingers that required stitching by Dr McLean. 5 February 1912 (Reported by Hunter, Madigan, Ninnis, mention only of the injury by Mawson, not the treatment.)

Surgery on dog "Caruso" by Drs McLean and Whetter. 7 March 1912. (Reported by Hunter, Madigan, Mawson, Ninnis, and Stillwell.)

Frank Stillwell suffered a whitlow on his hand requiring surgical lancing and treatment significant enough to warrant anaesthesia. Surgery 7 June 1912 by Drs McLean and Whetter. (Reported by Hunter, Mawson, Ninnis, and Stillwell.)

McLean himself needed two teeth removed requiring anaesthesia. Surgery by Dr Whetter, assisted by Hunter. 28 July 1912. (Reported by Hunter, Madigan, Ninnis, Stillwell, and McLean.)

Mawson's medical condition on his return. From 8 February 1913. (Reported by Mawson only.)

Jeffryes' mental condition, from July 1913. (Reported by Mawson, Madigan and McLean.)

McLean, as Chief Medical Officer, would have been considered doctor in charge of five of these six cases, yet only *one* of these cases is mentioned in his diary. That is Jeffryes' mental condition.[140] McLean does record the case where he was the *patient*, not the doctor, in his diary.[141]

This lends support to my suggestion that McLean was not generally in the habit of including patient notes in his personal diary. Therefore an absence of comment about Mawson's condition does not necessarily have any significance at all.

McLean did write the following about Mawson in the AAE Scientific Reports:

> *Dr Mawson during his eventful and tragic journey lived for nearly two months on dogs meat and a very scanty ration. He suffered from starvation primarily, though he relates that he had cutaneous eruptions accompanied by marked desquamation of the skin and the loss of hair. For some time after arriving at the Hut, his digestion was impaired and he had a partiality for farinaceous foods, fruit, and eggs.[142]*

This is independent verification of Mawson's condition written by the only medically qualified witness to his condition on return to the Huts.

Madigan's diary makes no mention of Mawson's condition at all except to characterise his only activity as follows – "Mawson eats."[143]   From both Mawson's and Madigan's diaries it is also clear that Mawson does more than his share of cooking at this time. It would hardly be unexpected for someone who has just survived nearly two months of starvation to be more than a little fixated on food.

I think Madigan was so self-absorbed and embittered by this time that I doubt he gave any thought at all to either Mawson's physical or mental condition.

There is another revealing comment from McLean, included as part of his discussion of the human will in the Expedition Scientific Reports:

> *But the trail leads unerringly to danger. And danger, once viewed frontwise with open eyes, vanishes to the contingency of every day. The experience of small perils is the education to a bland contemplation of horror in its just actuality. The habit of many days has ceased to be mere adventure. It is when that habit is rudely broken by the fell shock of calamity that the slumbering sea of volition boils up to prove its strength.*

There is the vision of a figure stumbling companionless, dragging on through the changeless days of threshing, settling snow drift. He has learnt in times long past the lessons of adversity, the grand solitude of self-reliance. He is impelled to stumble on, sinking in the yielding beds of downy snow – so white and pure, yet so relentless in its mockery of human suffering! Hands and feet numb to the flapping gusts of the sheeting blizzard; yet the heart palpitates hot in the will-driven frame of the man who fights for the life still sweet to self, who fights for a life in the service of others.[144]

These do not strike me as the words of a man who had any doubt about what Mawson claimed to have suffered.

13

Alone on Skis?

If Mertz didn't have to haul the sledge with Mawson, he would have found it easy going on his skis. Indeed, had he been without the impediment of Mawson, Mertz might have been able to use his survival skills from the Swiss Alps to ski all the way back to the hut.[145]

This is a novel suggestion, but in my opinion, not a realistic one. The accident occurred approximately 300 miles from the Hut. Even if Mertz was able to cover an extraordinary 30 to 50 miles per day on his 1911 model skis, he would still have taken between 6 and 10 days to reach safety. He would need to eat, drink and rest during that time, and navigate his way.

Such a feat might just be possible today for a person using a modern tent and sleeping bag, modern stove, and GPS. The equipment available today is much more compact and could possibly fit in a backpack or a small current design sledge, designed to be towed by someone on skis. Add a sail, and the right wind and terrain, and it would be relatively easy. Modern travellers using parasails have been known to cover as much as 140 miles (226 km) in a very long day when the wind conditions and surface are perfect.[146] Even without sails, Castrission and Jones covered up to 31 miles per day on skis with light loads during their return from the Pole in 2012.[147]

However, Mertz did not have modern equipment. He had a heavy reindeer skin sleeping bag, there was only one makeshift tent, and one primus stove. In my opinion, he is unlikely to have even been able to carry what he would have needed to survive for more than one night.

If Mertz had taken that equipment, it would have meant certain death for Mawson. When you consider the speculation and criticism that Mawson has suffered about possible cannibalism, when he clearly did not abandon his dying companion, it is interesting to contemplate what might have been said of Mertz had he abandoned Mawson alive and uninjured, and somehow survived himself. The man would in all likelihood have become a complete pariah.

Such an action would also appear to have been completely out of character for Mertz. Ninnis, the man who had come to know him best wrote this of him:

> *Quite the hardest and strongest man amongst us, he is splendid for all work under trying conditions. He is plucky well over the verge of*

recklessness, and does not know what is to fear anything. He is as generous and unaffected as it is possible for a fellow to be, and as broad minded. One could not, by any stretch of the imagination, picture him even contemplating a low or petty action. ... He is one of the finest, if not the finest fellow I have ever met, and knowing him and others on this show, notably Mawson, Bick, Madigan, Hurley etc, has done more for me mentally, morally and physically, than anything else could have done.[148]

Importantly, Day quotes Mertz's diary "have to stick close together, Mawson and I."[149]

From all accounts it seems that Mertz was a decent and honourable man, who would never even have contemplated abandoning Mawson. Note however, that this essay is written in the absence of further knowledge of Mertz's diary, which is written in German. There is a transcript only, held in South Australia, and it has not yet been published.

14

Legacy

Mawson's Far Eastern sledging journey failed to meet its objective and turned into a disaster of epic proportions, but the same cannot be said of the expedition as a whole. Nevertheless Day has stated that the expedition "had been grand it its conception, but poorly executed and limited in its immediate results."[150]

There were reasons why the expedition seemed to almost sink without trace as far as public perception was concerned, and they did not have anything to do with the quality of the enterprise itself. It was really just a case of very bad timing. While the AAE was in progress, the South Pole had been achieved, and Scott had died trying, becoming a dead hero in the process and receiving massive public adulation. Mawson's venture was never going to gain attention due to any single big achievement, because that was not the aim of it. Ironically, the tragedy that occurred, and Mawson's narrow winning through against the odds, probably gave him a better chance at publicity, and higher book and film sales than would have been the case if his journey had been completely successful and all the expedition's goals had been achieved. The chances of covering his costs might have been even better if Mawson had died, thereby making it potentially a tragedy to rival that of Scott. If Mawson did add somewhat to the drama of the events of his return journey for the published account, as Day has claimed, can we really blame him? It is his story alone to tell.[151]

Day is highly critical of Mawson's changing accounts of the story of pulling himself out of the crevasse. Mawson clearly did not invent the story purely for the purposes of increasing his book sales, since it is detailed at some length in his diary, so we must assume that it actually happened. However, because the diary gives a bare bones account, and the book a more embellished and more highly dramatic one, Mawson is criticised for making himself out to be a hero.

At the end of the Expedition, Mawson is estimated to have been personally in debt to the amount of £3,700 after the sale of the *Aurora*.[152] That is, more than ten times his University of Adelaide annual salary. Faced with such significant debt, as well as the immediate prospect of setting up a home and supporting a wife, can he really be blamed for writing as dramatic an account as possible, in order to gain sales. He would hardly be the first or last person who had done so. If Mawson had suddenly invented the story purely for the book, that would be a different matter entirely.

I find it particularly interesting that Day criticises Mawson for exaggerating the drama of an apparently true event, yet sees no problem himself with making highly controversial allegations about the conduct of a much admired, and long dead, historical figure on the basis of little or no actual evidence.

Publication of *The Home Of The Blizzard* was delayed due to the imminent war, and ultimately sales were disappointingly low. While the attention span of the general public may have been a bit longer in 1915 than it is now, clearly, another Polar venture that was focussed on mapping and science just did not rate in the eyes of the general public, when compared to the achievement of the Pole, the death of Scott, and the even more massive tragedy unfolding in the First World War.

Also noteworthy is that contrary to Madigan's expressed opinion that the expedition was about "Mawson first and the rest nowhere"[153] Mawson's published account gives a great deal of credit and space to the other sections of the expedition, including that of Madigan. In *The Home Of The Blizzard*, there are chapters devoted to the journeys lead by Madigan, Bage, Stillwell and Bickerton, Captain John King Davis and the *Aurora* crew, Frank Wild's western party, and the Macquarie Island party. Mawson states in his introduction "I wish to assure the various authors of my appreciation of their contributions and hope that someday they will themselves publish a fuller account of their adventures."[154] These chapters take up a full 42% of the narrative pages.[155]

Mawson cannot do anything right as far as Day is concerned. In this case he criticises Mawson for putting his name alone on the book when "most of it was written by other members of the expedition."[156] I am sure that had the book not included such chapters, and given due credit to all of the other members of the expedition, that would have been grounds for criticism as well.

The members of Mawson's expedition fared considerably better in this regard than did some members of Scott's expedition. The published account of Scott's last expedition contains scarcely a mention of Victor Campbell's Northern Party and their extraordinary story, although selection of material for publication was hardly Scott's responsibility, since he was dead.[157]

The scientific legacy of the Australasian Antarctic Expedition is another matter entirely. The immediate results may have been "limited" as Day suggests, but that was due to the fact that within six months of Mawson's return the war had broken out, and that was hardly Mawson's fault.

Results need to be published to be of value, and here Mawson really struggled, for many years. Following the war, Mawson could not afford to finance publication himself, and he struggled to get government funding, so although publication started in 1918, all twenty two volumes were not completed until 1947. Publication was only made possible with the support of the New South Wales Government, and its printing office, after a deal made with the South Australian Government fell through following a change of government. The significant amount of AAE document holdings in the Mitchell

Library and NSW museums was given in exchange for this assistance.[158]

The results themselves however, have proved to be of enormous value, and this expedition did more than any other of the era to advance scientific knowledge of the Antarctic.[159]

15

History, Speculation or Spin

There is usually more than one way to interpret events. In modern parlance interpreting events in a way that favours your own position is known as "spin". We should be very alert to this; after all, our politicians give us little else, and daily newspapers and television programs are full of it. Day finds just about every way he can to put a negative spin on everything Mawson said or did.

For example:
   Early in the sledging journey on 18 November 1912, Mawson wrote in his diary:
   "I did 2½ mile jog trot, leading after lunch, and did not feel it, so am getting into form".[160]

Circumstances: Eighth day of sledging journey, three days of which had been spent confined to the tent due to weather.

Day's version: (I have highlighted words I consider to be spin in bold.) After referring to Mertz taking the lead on skis in the morning Day writes:
   Mawson seems to have regarded it as a reflection on his own physique and **rose to the challenge**. *After lunch, he replaced Mertz in the lead. Not being adept at skiing, Mawson did a 'jog trot' for two and a half miles, noting* **with satisfaction**, *that he 'did not feel it, so am getting into form'.* **He was determined not to be outdone**.[161]

There is none of this sense of challenge or competition with his companions in Mawson's original entry. Professional historians should be carefully looking for the spin, and analysing it to determine what might or might not be the truth of the situation, rather than creating it.

And again:

Day writes of Mawson's journey, on 13 December 1912, referring to the area he hoped to map, to join up the unexplored area, with land sighted from the ship on Scott's expedition:

*He had estimated that point on the coast to be 350 miles from the hut, and he **must have realised** by now that it was beyond their ability to reach it.*[162]

Mawson's diary entry makes absolutely no mention of his planned date for turnaround. In *The Home Of The Blizzard* on 14 December, the day of the crevasse accident, Mawson wrote, "We were a happy party that morning as we revelled in the sunshine and laid plans for a final dash eastwards before turning our faces homewards." There is no mention however, of how long that final dash was planned to last. Three or four more days outbound with lightened loads may well have been achievable, and still not put them beyond a safe turnaround date.

We do not know what Mawson was planning or what his thoughts were, because he does not tell us. So why does Day use the word "must" in this context? While it is possible that Mawson did indeed think that way, the word "must" gives an incorrect impression.

There are many ways for historians to write without giving the impression of definite knowledge that is simply not there. Phrases and words such as: it is likely that, may have, possibly, probably.

Historians should take great care not to give the reader the impression of fact, when what they are writing is their own analysis or speculation.

16

The Character of Mawson

There is much that can be learned about the real Mawson from the recently released material. It should come as no surprise to anyone that he had at least his fair share of the common human flaws and failings—exactly like the rest of us. Flaws that several members of the expedition observed and recorded in their diaries. Mawson was certainly no saint, and that would already have been apparent to all from a reading of his own diaries, available in print since 1988. Mawson's reputation has been that of an austere, somewhat aloof, and demanding, leader who suffered neither fools nor idlers gladly. Most of that is borne out by Mawson's own testimony.

Mawson's priority was always the good of the expedition, and he worked himself as hard, if not harder than anyone. Mawson clearly liked some people more than others, and the same was undoubtedly true in reverse. This sounds exactly like the behaviour you will find in just about any workplace situation in normal life. Those Mawson particularly disliked were the individuals he thought were lazy and not contributing their best efforts. His feelings about Whetter and Close particularly are often mentioned in his diaries. Those of Hunter, Madigan and Stillwell reveal that this was not just Mawson's opinion. Close was frequently the butt of everyone's jokes,[163] and no-one other than Ninnis seemed to like Whetter very much. Ninnis thought Whetter was just "hopelessly misunderstood, particularly by Mawson."[164]

Mawson's emphasis on continual work was the major part of the cause of the conflict with Whetter, but it was also something that he considered necessary for the benefit of all. Not only to progress the aims of the expedition, but to stop the malaise of boredom and inactivity from setting in under the extraordinarily difficult conditions in which they found themselves.

Mawson did remain separate from the men to some extent, and he had his own cubicle. Riffenburgh states;

> this was because, as well as being a private man, he had learned from Shackleton the importance of a leader not being lodged in the main room, so that the men would not feel constrained by his presence.[165]

No doubt this is partly true, and common to many expeditions of the era, each of which were a reflection of their respective time and society. Victor

Campbell's Northern Party on Scott's Last Expedition, when trapped in an ice cave for a whole winter, famously divided it up metaphorically into the traditional naval Ward Room for the officers and scientists, and the Mess Deck for the lower ranks, and all agreed not to officially 'hear' anything said on the other side of the invisible wall.[166]

The AAE was considerably more 'colonial' and democratic in character than Scott's more naval style of expedition, or even that of Shackleton, which still maintained class distinctions. There was no differentiation between 'officers' and 'men' on the AAE. This is particularly demonstrated by the fact that there was no dedicated cook on any of the three bases, with each man in turn, including Mawson, taking duty as cook, messman, and night watchman, (there were some exceptions for those with scientific duties). This is a tradition still honoured today on Australian bases, where although they now have professional chefs, everyone, including the station leader, takes a turn at being 'slushy', the modern equivalent of messman, and relief cook, so the chef can have a day off.[167]

While remaining very much the leader, the recently published diaries also show that Mawson was far from being completely aloof. Hunter's diary indicates that he did relax from about March, "The Doctor is becoming freer with us now and is joking and punning the whole day long".[168] Mawson did not keep himself entirely out of the fun, games and practical jokes either, since according to Hunter he was an active participant in winding up Close about the dangers of the acetylene lighting system,[169] and instigated the raid on Hurley and Hunter's Chocolate Bank.[170] Perhaps he was not *quite* as isolated and austere as had previously been thought.

Mawson's manner seems to have occasionally annoyed other expedition members also. Hunter noted that Mawson could be a bit of a know it all:

> It is one of the Doc's worst traits to speak dogmatically of subjects of which he has only a surface knowledge.[171]

Stillwell was also particularly frustrated by Mawson's tendency to vacillation. After confusing and frequently changing instructions about who was to be cook for the day, Stillwell wrote:

> Seems hard to fit in with a leader who changes his mind three times in a morning.[172]

Mawson was parsimonious, to the point of being mean and inconsiderate. The instruction that everyone would have to pay for their cables to home during the second winter was the cause of considerable and probably justified resentment, no matter how stretched the finances of the expedition were.[173]

Mawson occasionally let his temper get the better of him. On 24 June 1912 Stillwell wrote:

> DM had a very sore head this morning. Dad McLean was nightwatchman

and had managed to let the hut temperature down to 30° during the night and it was 32° when we turned out of bunks. So he consequently felt a bit chilly and vented a bit of his chilliness on Dad. After breakfast we went round looking for biff and pitched into Hodgeman and myself.[174]

Ninnis was scathing about Mawson's refusal to let himself and Mertz capture and kill enough seals to feed the dogs adequately:

Had we only been allowed to kill seals when we had the chance, the dogs could have had ample good food and would now be fattening up in preparation for sledging; as it is they are getting daily thinner. It was the worst mistake that has been made since we came here.[175]

But there was considerable praise from some of the men too. Although he did not have an individual scientific program, Mawson seems to have assisted everyone. Some appreciated the help, perhaps others did not. Hunter wrote:

I cannot praise the Doc too much for the assistance he has given me. He does all the hard bullocky work and yesterday sacrificed all other work for the dredging.[176]

Hunter's work had been particularly limited by the circumstances, and it appears that Mawson was especially keen to ensure that he had as much opportunity as possible to achieve some results.

Mawson certainly was not perfect. He had character flaws, just as we all do. Can we honestly expect that anyone's character would emerge unscathed from the publication of four diaries (so far) detailing minute daily observations made by colleagues living in close confinement, and extremely difficult circumstances, over an extended period?

17

Later Expeditions

Day makes very little mention of it in *Flaws In The Ice*, but Mawson went south twice more on the two BANZARE voyages during the summers of 1929-30 and 1930-31. This omission by Day is somewhat surprising in this context since Mawson's very public conflicts with the ship's captains on both voyages provide many further opportunities for criticism of Mawson.

These expeditions were very different in character to the AAE, and took place for very different reasons. Following the first world war, the land grab for control of Antarctica was starting in earnest. Britain had formally annexed the Falkland Island dependency (1908) and the Ross Sea Dependency (1923 – delegated to New Zealand), but had not formally claimed the area south of Australia explored by the AAE, despite the parties of both Mawson and Wild raising flags and making claims. France had claimed Adelie Land, and now there were significant fears that the Norwegians would pursue claims in the area regarded as belonging to Britain/Australia following the AAE.

The BANZARE expeditions were undertaken with three aims, firstly the political imperative of claiming the territory for Britain, on the understanding that it would be delegated to Australia. Secondly, evaluation of the prospects of commercial activities such as whaling for Australia, and only thirdly, the conduct of scientific investigations.

Mawson was appointed as expedition leader, with Davis as second in command. As Australia's most renowned Antarctic explorer, Mawson was probably the obvious choice to lead. He was however, in many ways precisely the wrong man for the job, since these expeditions were ship-based. There had already been a considerable level of conflict between himself and Davis during the return voyage of the *Aurora* in 1914. The demands of the explorer and the ship's captain are frequently incompatible.

The unusual command structure devised for BANZARE put both Davis and Mawson in invidious positions. Although Davis was the ship's master, he was not technically in command of the ship while Mawson was aboard. Davis had only the right to veto Mawson's decisions if he believed it necessary for the safety of the ship. Davis clearly hated the situation:

> *"It is impossible to make a man who is not a seaman, realize that ships have to be handled with prudence."* [177]

Perhaps Mawson thought this structure would be sufficient to prevent the conflict that had arisen on his previous voyage with Davis.

In his biography of Mawson, Philip Ayres has called this "divided command."[178] Personally, I side with Davis here, it was an intolerable position for him to be put in. Both Mawson and Davis by this time were men in their late forties, of considerable reputation and position, and undoubtedly with correspondingly substantial egos. Mawson had experience of being in command of men, but he was not qualified to be in command of a ship, and in my opinion his position should have been subordinate to Davis's in all cases concerning the navigation and management of the ship. Mawson stated that he would not have found that acceptable, so under those circumstances, the expedition was sailing into turbulent waters from the minute it left the dock in Cape Town.[179] It therefore comes as no surprise that the clashes between the Mawson and Davis were frequent, public, and seemingly irreconcilable. Davis resigned at the end of the first voyage.

The situation was little better on the second voyage. MacKenzie, the first officer on the first voyage was promoted to captain. Perhaps Mawson hoped he would be more pliable than Davis, but a similar problems occurred under his command.[180] This indicates to me that Mawson's demands were in all likelihood unreasonable at times, and incompatible with the Captain's absolute responsibility for the lives and safety of all on board, and for the safety of the *Discovery*, which was on loan from the British government.

Day contends that Mawson had shown himself to be a poor leader, a poor organizer, a poor decision maker during the AAE, and therefore responsible for leading his men to their deaths. If that was true, then surely everyone concerned with the AAE would have been aware of it, and would have had doubts about Mawson's suitability for further appointment as expedition leader.

If his faults were indeed so glaring – would anyone in a position of power have entrusted him with the command of two further expeditions? It would surely have been easy enough to respect Mawson's previous leadership, and his public standing, by appointing him to the organizing committee, but quietly sidelining him from the actual expedition by appointing another, probably younger, man to such a rigorous command.

Would anyone within the scientific communities – where Mawson was well known – have ever volunteered to go on an expedition under his leadership if his abilities as a scientist, organizer or leader were in serious doubt?

Would Frank Hurley, Morton Moyes, Alec Kennedy and even John King Davis, have agreed to sail with Mawson for a second or third time if they did not respect or trust him? Davis had clashed with Mawson on the final return voyage of the AAE, yet he still undertook to command the *Discovery*, even under the wretched conditions imposed upon him.

Would Percy Corell, and the person who disliked Mawson most, Cecil Madigan, have stated to the press their willingness to go on the expedition if there was a place for them, if they thought Mawson was likely to recklessly endanger everyone's lives?[181]

Fifteen years had passed since the conclusion of the AAE, but it would seem that no-one had any qualms about either appointing Mawson to lead BANZARE, or going with him on the expeditions. If Mawson's contemporaries did not doubt him, then the grounds for criticism of Mawson's leadership more than 100 years later would appear to be very shaky.

I can only conclude that Day does not mention BANZARE in any detail in *Flaws In The Ice* because the fact that Mawson was indeed trusted to lead, and men were willing to participate in it, does not fit in with his theories.

18

Conclusion

Dr David Day has written a sensational page turner of a book that creates an image of Mawson significantly at odds with most other published accounts. But is he right?   Is it possible to rescue the truth from the crevasse between Day's view and the more traditional one based on Mawson's own writings?

When reading accounts of all the expeditions of this era, it is easy to criticise them for their apparent amateurishness, and what we perceive as their haphazard approach to safety. But we are looking at them with modern eyes, and it is much harder to view them by contemporary standards. We must remember that they truly were the pioneers of the exploration of the last continent.   Early attempts at anything new frequently don't stand up well to the scrutiny of time.

Rather than being "inexperienced" as Day contends, I have shown that Mawson in fact had considerable Antarctic experience. Much more than either Scott, Shackleton or Amundsen did at the time they each led their respective first expeditions. In my opinion Mawson was the most suitable, and the most qualified Australian to lead the AAE.

Day has stated the Mawson's "overweening ambition" and "poor decision making" caused the deaths of his companions. His program was certainly ambitious, and he was undoubtedly an ambitious man, but the fact that the vast majority of the planned expedition was successfully completed shows that organising, funding and managing such a venture was not beyond Mawson's capability.   The AAE was as well funded and as well equipped as other expeditions of the time. No one suffered injury due to failure or inadequacy of the facilities, equipment and supplies provided. The only possible exception to this was the use of skis, which Mawson saw as something of a novelty, and not as a safer and more efficient means of travel. In this respect, Mawson was a product of his culture and experience.

On the sledging journeys, Mawson's margins of safety were definitely very thin, and travel was risky. The same could be said for almost every expedition of this era. Scott and his party managed to come to grief on what should have been the least risky of all Antarctic sledging journeys, since the only unknown part of it was the final 97 miles across the plateau to the Pole. His risks should have been considerably more manageable for being known, whereas Mawson was exploring entirely uncharted territory. Mawson had no idea what conditions or terrain he might encounter in the area he had chosen to explore.

Amundsen is generally regarded as the master polar traveller of the era. Yet he took a huge risk in establishing his base camp on the Ross Ice Shelf at the Bay of Whales. Nothing went wrong, so Amundsen emerged as the outstanding example of polar travel expertise and efficiency. Opinions would have been very different if the ice shelf had calved and his base had gone out to sea. So was Amundsen taking a reasonable and calculated risk in locating his base, or needlessly jeopardising the lives of his entire party? It is all a matter of interpretation.

Mawson's own sledge journey with Ninnis and Mertz was much more modest in scope than the journey he had previously completed on the BAE with David and McKay. The planned 700 mile round trip with dogs should have been within their capacity and resources to achieve. Madigan, and therefore Day, condemn Mawson for travelling in an area of extensive crevassing. That may well have been true, but crevasses were also found much further inland, and even within close proximity to the Huts. Virtually nowhere on ice can be assumed to be completely free of crevasses. Travel in Antarctica was not safe then, and it is still not without risk today. The only way to completely avoid crevasses in Antarctica is to never venture onto the ice.

Mawson's party started with three sledges, and reduced to two as food and fuel were consumed. But they had only one tent, a spare tent cover, and one stove. There was virtually no redundancy in vital equipment, and the supplies were not evenly divided between the sledges. They could not afford to lose either sledge, and so the loss of Ninnis and his sledge in the crevasse left Mawson and Mertz in dire straits. The same thing could easily have happened to any other party on any other expedition. The consequences would have been almost immediately fatal to any party hauling a single sledge, or any party that lost their only tent or stove. Amundsen was the only one who travelled with anything approaching a reasonable safety margin. As I have detailed, I believe that Mawson and Mertz were significantly better off than they would have been if Mawson's sledge carrying the cooking stove, was the one that was lost.

Most controversially, Day has suggested that Mawson cut the rations to an unnecessarily low level in the hope that Mertz would die first, leaving more food for himself, an act tantamount to deliberate murder. I have shown that the rations were cut to a level that I believe is consistent with ensuring that there was some food available for two men for the entire amount of time that the journey back to the Huts might take. Day asserts that Mawson's increased food consumption, and changed pattern of consumption, following Mertz's death is evidence for his theory. However, a different interpretation is in fact far more likely. After Mertz died there was twice as much food available for Mawson, and it would be completely unreasonable to expect him not to eat it, and not to review his rationing system due to the changed circumstances.

What cannot be argued, even by Day, is that Mawson's Australasian Antarctic Expedition was a failure. This expedition contributed vastly more than any other single venture of the era to geographical and scientific knowledge about Antarctica. The scientific results were of great significance, not least because they explored and charted a huge amount of previously unknown territory, and even Day admits that they are still in use today as a basis for comparison with current results and research.[182] The fame of the expedition was simply eclipsed by even more dramatic events that captured the public imagination. Events including Amundsen's achievement of the South Pole, Scott's death, Shackleton's later epic of survival on the ITAE, the sinking of the Titanic, and most importantly the First World War.

The aim of Mawson's expedition was always scientific and geographical exploration, so in all probability it would never have captured the public imagination in quite the same way as an attempt at the South Pole. The modern equivalent of the early exploration of Antarctica is surely the exploration of the Moon. Everyone knows about Apollo 11, and probably Apollo 13, because that mission was a dramatic failure, and the subject of several books and a highly successful movie. However, only the enthusiasts could tell you very much, if anything, about the other five moon landing missions, or even give you the name of the third man to set foot on the moon.[183] Yet those missions were extremely valuable, and made far greater contributions to current scientific knowledge about the Moon than did Apollo 11.

What Mawson personally endured, along with other members of his team, in order to achieve those scientific results can only be imagined by us today, aided by the insights gained from the expedition diaries. Mawson's trek back to the Huts, both with Mertz, and finally alone, and the sheer creeping awfulness of the second wintering show his immense personal endurance, strength and courage.

It is surprising to find that this real life story of tragedy, endurance, survival and triumph against the odds is not better known today, especially amongst Australians. Most people I have ear-bashed about Mawson over the years are amazed to hear the details. For many, he was just the guy wearing the woolly balaclava on the old $100 note, and even that memory is fading now that the currency design has changed.

There were many 'flaws' in the ice during the AAE, but not all of them were Mawson's. Each of the men of the expedition had their own individual failings. Their flaws, as well as Mawson's are now evident for all to see in the published diaries, and we are gradually discovering a fuller, more detailed, and much more human picture of Mawson, and all of the men of the expedition.

Mawson certainly did not have the same charismatic personality as Shackleton. He was first, last and always a scientist, and perhaps not a born leader of men. Most of the critical remarks made about him by his men should not be unexpected, especially when due consideration is given to the extremely difficult circumstances of their origin. In later years it was clear that many of the AAE men greatly admired Mawson and recalled their time on the expedition with much fondness.[184]

The great triumph of the Expedition is that despite the flaws of each individual, and the extremely adverse conditions they encountered, they still managed to work together to carry out an outstandingly successful program of exploration and scientific observations, despite the tragic deaths of Ninnis and Mertz.

Day's controversial analysis is also a seriously flawed work. His view of Mawson displays an extremely negative bias. In my opinion, its main problem is that there is insufficient evidence to support many of the author's most controversial criticisms and theories. However, if his sensational character assassination attempt brings Mawson's story back to current attention then that may be a good thing in some ways. I sincerely hope that his ideas are not accepted as the whole story by readers new to the material, and that they too think critically about Day's theories and read further for themselves.

My own admiration for what Mawson and all the men of the AAE achieved remains undiminished by Dr Day's extremely critical account. The research he has inspired me to complete has meant that if anything, my admiration is strengthened. These courageous men did what none of us today can do – they ventured into one of the last completely unknown areas on this planet, and did all that was humanly possible to map, explore, systematically record and observe it, and bring home those records and samples. Despite everything that both Antarctica and human nature threw against them, their achievements were extraordinary. Their stories deserve to be better known, and their success celebrated.

Afterword

David Day's next project after *Flaws In The Ice* was a biography of Paul Keating, who served as Prime Minister of Australia from December 1991 to March 1996.   Unlike Mawson, Paul Keating is still very much alive, and remains active in public life.

In this unauthorised biography, Day alleges that Mr Keating suffered from dyslexia. Mr Keating has vigorously denied this in the press.[185] It has now been reported that Mr Keating sued Day and his publishers HarperCollins. The case has been settled, with Day and his publishers issuing a formal apology, paying Mr Keating's legal costs, pulping unsold copies, and agreeing to significant amendments in any further printings.

Mr Keating is reported to have written "The worst of it is you have not a shred of credible evidence for the claims you have made …"[186]

Notes

1. Mornement, A & Riffenburgh, B *Mertz and I... The Antarctic Diary of Belgrave Edward Sutton Ninnis* The Erskine Press 2014.   30 January 2012 p. 233
    Subsequent references in Notes listed as *"Ninnis Diary"*
2. Roosevelt, T Excerpt from the speech "Citizenship In A Republic" delivered at the Sorbonne, in Paris, France on 23 April, 1910
3. Day, D *Flaws In The Ice* Scribe 2013 p. 3
4. Mawson, D *The Home Of The Blizzard* Hodder & Stoughton Popular Edition   1930 p. 324
5. Day, D *Flaws In The Ice* p. 3
6. Day, D *Flaws In The Ice* p. 3
7. Madigan, C T *Madigan's Account: The Mawson Expedition* J W Madigan (ed) Wellington Bridge Press 2012 Subsequent references in Notes listed as "Madigan Diary"
8. Evans, R Documentary "The Kid Stays in the Picture" 2002 http://en.wikiquote.org/wiki/Robert_Evans
9. Fiennes, R *Cold* Simon & Schuster 2013 p. 138
10. Fiennes, R *Cold* p. 186
11. Trip Advisor - Reviews of Mawson's Huts Replica Museum. http://www.tripadvisor.com.au/Attraction_Review-g255097-d5605486-Reviews-Mawson_s_Hut_Replica_Museum-Hobart_Tasmania.html
12. Mawson, D *The Home Of The Blizzard* p. 55
13. Ninnis Diary 1 August 1912 p.363
14. Learmonth, E & Tabakoff , J *No Mercy* Text Publishing 2013, McPhee, J & Charles, J (eds) *Human Health and Performance Risks of Space Exploration Missions* NASA 2009 p. 16
15. Learmonth, E & Tabakoff , J *No Mercy* p. 94
16. Hunter, J G *Rise & Shine: Diary of John George Hunter* J M Hunter (ed) Hunter House Publications 2011. Entry for 27 August 1912 p. 135 Subsequent references in Notes listed as *"Hunter Diary"*
17. McLean, A Diary Mitchell Library MLMSS382 Typed Narrative 4 June 1912
18. Ninnis Diary 4 May 1912 p. 300
19. Hunter Diary 8 February 1913 p. 194
20. Madigan Diary 19 November 1911 p. 3
21. Madigan Diary 21 November 1911 p. 5
22. Madigan Diary 23 November 1911 p. 6, 20 December 1911 p. 31
23. Madigan Diary 10 December 1911 p.20
24. Madigan Diary 26 May 1912 p. 181

25. Website: Australian Government   http://www.antarctica.gov.au/jobs/jobs-in-antarctica

26. Madigan Diary 5 April 1912   p. 145 "Dux Ipse" or "D.I."- The leader himself. Day and others have said that this was not meant to be flattering and was not used to Mawson's face. (*Flaws in the Ice* p. 84   Ayres, P *Mawson: A Life* p. 62) However, Ninnis reports in his diary that he baked a pie with "D I"on it for Mawson's birthday. (Ninnis Diary 5 May 1912 p. 301.) It would seem this nickname may not have been a secret from Mawson.

27. Madigan Diary p. 279   In this comment and many others Madigan states that he is not alone in his opinion about Mawson.

28. Madigan Diary 12 November 1912 p. 300

29. Madigan Diary 13 February 1912   p. 352

30. Madigan Diary 13 February 1912   p. 352

31. Madigan Diary 13 February 1912   p. 351

32. Travel across sea ice was potentially dangerous, since ice can rapidly break up and be blown out to sea. Two men of Shackleton's Ross Sea party died in 1916 crossing unstable ice. This is not to say that the area Madigan was travelling in was necessarily unsafe.

33. Hunter Diary   8 February 1913 p. 194

34. Hince, B (ed) *Still No Mawson, Frank Stillwell's Antarctic Diaries 1911-13*   8 February 1913   p. 223. Subsequent references in Notes listed as "*Stillwell Diary*"

35. McLean Diary 8 February 1913   ML MSS 382

36. Madigan Diary 12 March 1913   p. 365, 18 March 1913   p. 367

37. Madigan Diary 17 July 1913 p. 402

38. Madigan Diary 28 May 1913 p. 386

39. Madigan Diary 16 April 1913 p. 377

40. Jacka, & Jacka (eds) *Mawson's Antarctic Diaries* 26 May 1913 p. 192 Subsequent references in Notes listed as "*Mawson Diary*"

41. Madigan Diary 23 April 1913 p. 380

42. Madigan Diary 20 June 1913 p. 391

43. Madigan Diary 9 March 1913 p. 364

44. Madigan Diary 14, 16 , 28 February 1913 pp. 352 - 359

45. Madigan Diary 1 April, 21 April, 29 May 1913

46. Website: Sane Australia
http://www.sane.org/information/factsheets-podcasts/178-depression
http://www.sane.org/information/factsheets-podcasts/199-bipolar-disorder

47. Hunter Diary 31 May 1912, p. 90

48. Riffenburgh, B *Aurora* Erskine Press 2011

49. Riffenburgh, B   Personal communication 24 April 2015

50. Riffenburgh, B *Aurora*   pp. 424, 425

51. Madigan Diary 9 March 1913 p. 364

52. Newspaper Article:
WELCOME HOME. (1914, March 3). *The Advertiser* (Adelaide, SA : 1889 - 1931), p. 9. Retrieved from http://nla.gov.au/nla.news-article5418365

53. Parkin, L. W. 'Madigan, Cecil Thomas (1889–1947)', Australian Dictionary of Biography, National Centre of Biography, Australian National University, http://adb.anu.edu.au/biography/madigan-cecil-thomas-7455/text12985, published in hardcopy 1986
54. Ayres, P *Mawson: A Life* p. 231/2
55. Newspaper Articles:
   a) EXPLORING ANTARCTIC. (1928, September 12).News (Adelaide, SA : 1923 - 1954), p. 11 Edition: HOME EDITION. Retrieved from http://nla.gov.au/nla.news-article129166019
   b) ANTARCTIC EXPLORATION. (1928, September 27). *The Register*(Adelaide, SA : 1901 - 1929), p. 12. Retrieved from http://nla.gov.au/nla.news-article56764819
   c) MAWSON EXPEDITION. (1929, June 14).News(Adelaide, SA : 1923 - 1954), p. 1 Edition: HOME EDITION. Retrieved from http://nla.gov.au/nla.news-article129120267
   also
   Fletcher, H *Antarctic Days With Mawson* p. 224
56. Twidale CR, Parkin LW, Rudd, EA 'C T Madigan's Contributions to Geology in South and Central Australia' *Transactions of the Royal Society of South Australia* Vol 114 1990
57. Day, D *Flaws In The Ice* p. 2
58. Websites:
   http://www.coolantarctica.com/Antarctica%20fact%20file/History/Robert%20Falcon%20Scott.htm
   http://en.wikipedia.org/wiki/Discovery_Expedition
   http://www.coolantarctica.com/Antarctica%20fact%20file/History/Ernest%20Shackleton_Nimrod_expedition.htm
59. Mawson Diary 10 January 1910 p. 53
60. Mawson Diary January 1910 pp. 53-55
61. Ninnis Diary 23 July 1911 p127/128
62. Mawson, D *The Home Of The Blizzard* p. 135
63. Mawson, D *The Home Of The Blizzard* p. 212
64. Day, D *Flaws In The Ice* p. 157
65. Website: http://www.instructables.com/id/Survivals-Law-of-3/?ALLSTEPS
   There are numerous references for this "rule".
66. Mawson, D *The Home Of The Blizzard* p. 163
67. Mawson, D *The Home Of The Blizzard* pp. 135, 149,150
68. Castrission, J *Extreme South* Hachette Australia 2012 Kindle reference:1969
69. Website:
   http://en.wikipedia.org/wiki/Heroic_Age_of_Antarctic_ExplorationWikipedia
70. Day, D *Flaws In The Ice* p. 242
71. Ninnis Diary 15 July 1911 p. 123
72. Ninnis Diary 23 October 1912   p. 416
73. Kranz, E *Our Time* Essay published on: http://www.honeysucklecreek.net/last_days/index.html

74. Huntford, R *Scott and Amundsen* Abacus 1999 p. 413.
    Amundsen's Diary 31 October 1911
    http://sorpolen2011.npolar.no/en/diary-amundsen/1911-10-31.html
75. Hilary/Fuchs crossing, British Antarctic Survey 1965, Norwegian expedition
    1993 to name a few.
76. Day, D *Flaws In The Ice* p. 142
77. Ninnis Diary 17 September 1912 p 396
78. Website: http://www.titanic-titanic.com/lifeboats.shtml
79. Newspaper Article:
    HEROISM OF DR. MAWSON. (1913, April 19). *The Daily News* (Perth, WA :
    1882 - 1950), p. 6 Edition: THIRD EDITION. Retrieved from
    http://nla.gov.au/nla.news-article79838433
80. Day, D *Flaws In The Ice* p. 198
81. Ayres, P *Mawson: A Life* p. 78
    Just about every book on Mawson mentions the cannibalism suggestion. It is
    apparently based on suggestions made in the American press.
82. Day, D *Flaws In The Ice* p. 199
83. Mawson Diary 9 January 1913 p. 158
84. Mawson Diary 15 January 1913 p. 161
85. Mawson Diary 9 January 1913, p. 158 and 18 Jan, p. 162 for example.
86. Mawson Diary 15 December, 23 December, 28 December, 29 December, 30
    December 1912, 10 January, 1913
87. Mawson Diary 14 December, 1912 p 148
88. Mawson, D *The Home Of The Blizzard* p 170
89. Mawson Diary 4 January, 1912 p. 157
90. Mawson, D *The Home Of The Blizzard* p. 196
91. Mawson Diary 15 December 1912 p. 150, and 18 December 1912 p. 151.
92. Mawson Diary 4 January 1913 p. 157
93. Day, D *Flaws In The Ice* p. 163
94. Wikipedia: http://en.wikipedia.org/wiki/Rabbit_starvation
95. Day, D *Flaws In The Ice* Notes p. 281, compared with text p. 170
96. Day, D *Flaws In The Ice* p. 170
97. Day, D *Flaws In The Ice* p. 172
98. Mawson, D *The Home Of The Blizzard* p. 167
99. Mawson, D *The Home Of The Blizzard* p. 170
100. Shearman, D 'Vitamin A & Sir Douglas Mawson' *British Medical Journal* 4
     Feb 1978
101. Mawson, D *The Home Of The Blizzard* p. 167
102. Day, D *Flaws In The Ice* p. 162
103. Jarvis, T *Mawson: Life & Death in Antarctica* Miegunyah Press 2008 p. 222
104. Madigan Diary: For example, on Madigan's journey he states on Dec 4 that a
     week's rations over 8 days seems enough, but on Dec 8 that the ration does not
     satisfy.
105. Mawson, D *The Home Of The Blizzard* p. 143
106. Madigan Diary 17 November 2013 p. 303
107. Website: coep.pharmacy.arizona.edu/curriculum/tox_basics/toxhandouts.doc

108. Gonzales, L *Deep Survival: Who Lives, Who Dies & Why* Norton 2003.
    Extensive analysis of the importance of mental attitude in survival situations.
109. Day, D *Flaws In The Ice* p. 238
110. Madigan Diary 23 October 1912 p. 279
111. Mawson Diary 21 October 1912 p. 125
112. Madigan Diary 22 May 1913 p. 385
113. Madigan Diary   12 and 13 December 1912 p. 321,322
114. Jacka & Jacka   *Mawson's Antarctic Diaries* Allen & Unwin   1988
    Notes p. xxx
115. Shackleton, E *Heart Of The Antarctic* Vol II p. 73-222
116. Madigan Diary 23 November 1911   p. 7
117. Madigan Diary 19 December 1911 p. 40,   4 January 1912   p. 52
118. Madigan Diary 23 October 1912   p. 279
119. Mythbusters 'Walk A Straight Line' Oct 12, 2011
    http://www.discovery.com/tv-shows/mythbusters/2011-episodes.htm
120. Crossley, L (ed) *Trial By Ice: The Antarctic Journals of John King Davis*
    Bluntisham Books & The Erskine Press 30 January 1913 p. 58
    Subsequent references in Notes listed as *"Davis Diary"*
121. Day, D *Flaws In The Ice*   p. 213
122. Mawson Diary   8 January 1913, p. 158
123. Newspaper article:
    DR. MAWSON'S CONFIDENCE IN SCOTT. *The Sydney Morning Herald*
    (NSW : 1842 - 1954) 30 Mar 1911: 9. Web. 1 Feb 2015
    <http://nla.gov.au/nla.news-   article15239239>
124. Madigan Diary   22 October 1912   p. 278
125. Madigan Diary 12 November 1912 p. 301
126. Madigan Diary : Duration of sledging journey 8 November 1912,
    to 16 January 1913 pp.   297-348
127. Day, D *Flaws In The Ice*   p. 109
128. Ninnis Diary 27 October 1912   p. 419
129. Day, D *Flaws In The Ice*   p. 218
130. Day, D *Flaws In The Ice*   p. 117
131. Day, D *Flaws In The Ice*   p. 215
132. Davis Diary 2 February 1913 p. 59
133. Madigan Diary 13 February 1913 p. 352
134. Davis Diary 1 February 1913 p. 59
135. Day, D *Flaws In The Ice*   p. 222
136. Day, D *Flaws In The Ice*   p. 226
137. Day, D *Flaws In The Ice*   p. 227
138. Mawson Diary   30 July 1913 p. 199
139. McLean, A Diary   Mitchell Library MLMSS382 Typed Narrative.
140. McLean, A Diary   Mitchell Library MLMSS382 Typed Narrative.
    11 July 1913
141. McLean, A Diary   Mitchell Library MLMSS382 Typed Narrative.
    28 July 1912
142. McLean, A "Bacteriological and other researches" *Australasian Antarctic*
    Expedition Scientific Reports Vol VII Part 4 p. 116

143. Madigan Diary   16 February 1913   p. 354
144. McLean, A "Bacteriological and other researches" *Australasian Antarctic Expedition Scientific Reports* Vol VII Part 4 p. 124
145. Day, D *Flaws In The Ice*   pp. 168 & 230
146. Butler, A   *Ice Tracks* The Erskine Press 2008   p. 69
147. Castrission, J *Extreme South* Expedition Notes
148. Ninnis, Diary 10 May 1912
149. Day, D *Flaws In The Ice*   p. 157 quotes this diary.
150. Day, D *Flaws In The Ice*   p. 278
151. Day, D *Flaws In The Ice*   pp. 203-205
152. Ayres, P *Mawson: A Life* p. 99
153. Madigan Diary 9 March 1913 p. 364
154. Mawson, D *The Home Of The Blizzard* p. vii
155. Mawson, D *The Home Of The Blizzard*   Hodder & Stoughton Popular Edition 1930
156. Day, D *Flaws In The Ice* p. 246
157. Scott, R.F, *Scott's Last Expedition*, John Murray 1923 (Cheap Edition)
158. Website: NSW State Records
    http://gallery.records.nsw.gov.au/index.php/galleries/people-of-interest/sir-douglas-mawson-blizzards-and-bureaucracy/
159. The AAE was more scientifically productive than any other single expedition both in terms of territory discovered, and its quantity of scientific publications.
    Scott NAE 1901-1904 - Published 10 volumes of reports, plus one of pictures.
    Mawson AAE 1911-1914 - Published 22 volumes of reports.
    Scott NAE 1901-1904 - Discovered 1050 miles, explored 200 miles
    Shackleton BAE - Discovered 1035, explored 300 miles
    Mawson AAE 1911-1914 - Discovered 1840 miles, explored 1720 miles
    Scott Terra Nova - Discovered 285 miles, explored 100 miles
    Source: Riffenburgh, B *Aurora* p. 421, 486
160. Mawson Diary 18 November 1912   p. 132
161. Day, D *Flaws In The Ice* p. 140
162. Day, D *Flaws In The Ice* p. 148
163. Hunter Diary 15 June 1912 p. 99
164. Ninnis Diary 24 September 1912 p. 397
165. Riffenburgh, B *Aurora* p. 129
166. King, HGR (Ed) *The Wicked Mate: The Antarctic Diary of Victor Campbell* The Erskine Press Bluntisham Books 1988   p. 129
167. Website: Australian Government   http://www.antarctica.gov.au/living-and-working/station-life-and-activities/station-duties-and-volunteer-positions/slushy-duties
168. Hunter Diary   4 March 1912 p. 46
169. Hunter Diary   24 April 1912 pp. 70, 74
170. Hunter Diary   1 May 1912 p. 81,   also   Madigan Diary p. 171
171. Hunter Diary   30 Sept 1912 p. 150
172. Stillwell Diary 25 Sept 1912 p. 149
173. Madigan Diary 29 May 1913   p. 387
174. Stillwell Diary 24 June 1912 p. 151

175. Ninnis Diary 21 July 1912 p.356
176. Hunter Diary 4 September 1912 p. 140
177. Davis Diary   2 December 1929, p 131
178. Ayres, P *Mawson: A Life* p.164
179. Ayres, P *Mawson: A Life* p.164
180. Ayres, P *Mawson: A Life* p.200, and
    Grenfell Price, A *The Winning of Australian Antarctica* p. 159
181. Newspaper articles:
    a) OLD COMRADES WILL JOIN MAWSON. (1929, March 1). *The Register News-Pictorial* (Adelaide, SA : 1929 - 1931), p. 8. Retrieved from
    http://nla.gov.au/nla.news-article53468437
    b) EXPLORING ANTARCTIC. (1928, September 12). *News* (Adelaide, SA : 1923 - 1954), p. 11 Edition: HOME EDITION. Retrieved from
    http://nla.gov.au/nla.news-article129166019
182. Day, D *Flaws In The Ice* p. 279
183. Website: Lunar & Planetary Institute
    http://www.lpi.usra.edu/lunar/missions/apollo.
    The third man on the moon was Pete Conrad, on 19 November 1969.
184. Ayres, P *Mawson: A Life* p. 254
185. Letter to the Editor *The Sydney Morning Herald* 3 February 2015
186. Newspaper Article:
    KEATING WINS HIS OWN HISTORY WAR   *The Sydney Morning Herald*
    9 May 2015.

Bibliography

Primary Sources

Crossley, L (ed) *Trial By Ice: The Antarctic Journals of John King Davis*, Bluntisham Books   The Erskine Press 1997

Fletcher, H *Antarctic Days With Mawson* Angus & Robertson 1984

Hince, B (ed) *Still No Mawson, Frank Stillwells Antarctic Diaries 1911-13* Australian Academy of Science   2012

Hunter, J M (ed) *Rise & Shine: Diary of John George Hunter* Hunter House Publications   2011

Hurley, F *Argonauts of the South* Putnam's 1925

Jacka, & Jacka (eds) *Mawson's Antarctic Diaries*, Allen & Unwin 1988

King, H G R (ed) *The Wicked Mate: The Antarctic Diary of Victor Campbell* The Erskine Press Bluntisham Books,   1988

Laseron, C F *South With Mawson* Australasian Publishing Company   1947

McLean, A   Diary   Unpublished   Mitchell Library   ML MSS 382

McLean, A "Bacteriological and other researches"   Australasian Antarctic Expedition Scientific Reports Vol VII Part 4

Mornement, A and Riffenburgh, B   *Mertz and I... The Antarctic Diary of Belgrave Edward Sutton Ninnis* The Erskine Press 2014

Madigan, J (ed) *Madigan's Account: The Mawson Expedition* Wellington Bridge Press   2012

Mawson, D *The Home Of The Blizzard* Hodder & Stoughton Popular Edition 1930

Scott, R.F. *Scott's Last Expedition* John Murray 1923

Shackleton, E *Heart Of The Antarctic* William Heinemann   1909

Secondary Sources

Ayres, P *Mawson: A Life* Miegunyah Press 1999

Butler, A *Ice Tracks* The Erskine Press 2008

Bickel, L *This Accursed Land* Macmillan 1977

Castrission, J *Extreme South* Hachette Australia 2012

Day, D *Flaws In The Ice* Scribe 2013

Fiennes, R *Cold* Simon & Schuster 2013

Fitzsimons, P *Mawson: And the ice men of the Heroic Age: Scott, Shackleton and Amundsen* Random House 2011

Gonzales, L *Deep Survival: Who Lives, Who Dies & Why* Norton 2003.

Grenfell Price, A *The Winning of Australian Antarctica* Angus & Robertson 1962

Huntford, R *Scott & Amundsen* Abacus 1999

Jarvis, T *Mawson: Life & Death in Antarctica* Miegunyah Press 2008

Learmonth, E & Tabakoff , J *No Mercy* Text Publishing 2013

Riffenburgh, B *Aurora* The Erskine Press 2011

Riffenburgh, B *Racing With Death* Bloomsbury 2008

Journals

Shearman, D 'Vitamin A & Sir Douglas Mawson' *British Medical Journal*
    4 Feb 1978
Lugg, D & Ayton, J 'In the footsteps of McLean, Jones and Whetter: 100 years of
    Australian Antarctic medical practice.' *Australian Antarctic Magazine* Issue 22
    2012
McPhee, J & Charles, J (eds) 'Human Health and Performance Risks of Space
    Exploration Missions' NASA 2009 p. 16
Twidale CR, Parkin LW, Rudd, EA 'C T Madigan's Contributions to Geology in
    South and Central Australia' *Transactions of the Royal Society of South
    Australia* Vol 114 1990

Film & Television

Hyneman, J & Savage, A Mythbusters 'Walk A Straight Line' Oct 12, 2011
    http://www.discovery.com/tv-shows/mythbusters/2011-episodes.htm
Jarvis, T *Mawson: Life & Death In Antarctica* DVD ABC 2007
Jones, J (Dir) *Crossing The Ice* DVD Quail Television 2012

Websites

Australian Government: http://www.antarctica.gov.au
Australian Dictionary of Biography: http://adb.anu.edu.au/biography/
Honeysuckle Creek: http://www.honeysucklecreek.net
Instructables: http://www.instructables.com
Lunar & Planetary Institute: http://www.lpi.usra.edu/lunar/missions/apollo
Sane Australia: http://www.sane.org
Trip Advisor: http://www.tripadvisor.com.au/Attraction_Review-g255097-
    d5605486-Reviews-Mawson_s_Hut_Replica_Museum-Hobart_Tasmania.html
Trove: trove.nla.gov.au Newspaper archives.
Titanic: http://www.titanic-titanic.com
University of Arizona: coep.pharmacy.arizona.edu/curriculum/tox_basics/
toxhandouts.doc
Wikipedia: http://en.wikipedia.org/wiki/Heroic_Age_of_Antarctic_Exploration

Picture Credits

With thanks to the Mawsons Huts Foundation for permission to use the second and
third photographs on page 94 and the photograph on the back cover. Many thanks
also to Tristan Higbee/The Aloof.com for permission to use his 'crevasse' photograph
on the cover.

All other photographs - with thanks to the publishers of *Mertz & I... The Antarctic
Diary of Belgrave Edward Sutton Ninnis* (ed) A. Mornement and B. Riffenburgh
(Erskine Press Norwich UK 2014) and with acknowledgement to *The Home of the
Blizzard* by Sir Douglas Mawson (J. Lippincott & Company, Philadelphia 1915).

Acknowledgements

This work would not have happened without the following people:

Firstly, and perhaps somewhat strangely, thanks to Dr David Day for getting me so steamed up over what he wrote about Mawson that I just had to do something about it. I've been on a wild research and writing ride the last few months and enjoyed it immensely.

Secondly, to indie author extraordinaire Hugh Howey, for providing the inspiration to publish my work, and the information to enable me to do it.

My dear friend and editor, Meghan Hayward, gave me gentle (and some not so gentle) nudges in the right direction, and pointed out my numerous beginner's writing errors, and some absolute howlers. The final form of this essay is *so* much better than the first one, thanks in very great part to her help and guidance. All remaining mistakes are mine alone.

Thanks to David Jensen of the Mawson's Huts Foundation for his support of this project, and to Andrew Jackson for some helpful suggestions. Thanks to Crispin de Boos of Erskine Press for permission to use the leading quote from Ninnis's diary. Thanks also to Dr Beau Riffenburgh for clarifying some points of his extensive research, for his introduction and for his support.

Last, but in no way least: enormous thanks to my beloved husband Greg, who has put up with me all these months, while I have been far too busy to do anything as mundane and boring as housework. I know that I will find another use for the magic bookshelf.

Karyn Maguire Bradford
Sydney
May 2015

MEMBERS OF THE AUSTRALASIAN ANTARCTIC EXPEDITION 1911-1914

Main Base Party – Commonwealth Bay			
Name	Age	Position	Qualifications
Dr Douglas Mawson *	30	Leader	D.Sc. (University of Adelaide), B.Sc. B.E (University of Sydney)
Lieutenant Robert Bage	23	Astronomer, Assistant Magnetician Recorder of Tides	B.E. (University of Melbourne) Lieutenant, Royal Engineers
Francis Bickerton	22	Motor Engineer, In charge of air-tractor sledge	Fellow of the Royal Geographical Society FRGS
John Close	40	Assistant Collector	FRGS
Percy Correll	19	Mechanic Assistant Physicist	Undergraduate student in Science, University of Adelaide.
Walter Hannam	26	Wireless Operator Mechanic	Diploma in Science, Sydney Technical College
Alfred Hodgeman	26	Cartographer Sketch artist	Articled architect, draughtsman, Government Works Department, Adelaide
John Hunter *	23	Biologist	B.Sc. University of Sydney Studying Medicine.
Frank Hurley	24	Photographer Cinematographer	
Sidney Jeffryes	27	Wireless Operator (second year only)	
Charles Laseron	25	Taxidermist Biological Collector	Diploma in Science, Sydney Technical College
Dr Archibald McLean	26	Chief Medical Officer Bacteriologist	Ch.M., M.B., B.A. University of Sydney
Cecil Madigan *	23	Meteorologist	B.E. University of Adelaide, Rhodes Scholarshipt o study at Oxford University
Dr Xavier Mertz	28	In Charge of Dogs	Doctor of Law University of Berne
Herbert Murphy	32	In Charge of Stores	Undergraduate student of history – Oxford University
Lieutenant Belgrave Ninnis *	23	In Charge of Dogs	Lieutenant, Royal Fusiliers
Frank Stillwell *	23	Geologist	B.E. Melbourne University
Eric Webb	22	Chief Magnetician	Associate Degree Civil Engineering University of Canterbury
Dr Leslie Whetter	29	Surgeon	M.B. Ch.B. Otago University

Western Base Party

Name	Age	Position	Qualifications
Frank Wild	38	Leader: Western Base	Member of Scott's *Discovery* expedition, and member of Shackleton's *Nimrod* expedition, including furthest south journey.
George Dovers	21	Surveyor	Licensed Surveyor
Charles Harrisson *	43	Biologist & Artist	
C Archibald Hoadley	24	Geologist	Degrees in Mining Engineering and Science, University of Melbourne
Dr S Evan Jones	24	Surgeon	MB.BS University of Sydney
Alexander L Kennedy	22	Magnetician	Science student, University of Adelaide
Morton Moyes	25	Meteorologist & Surveyor	B.Sc. University of Adelaide
Andrew Watson	24	Geologist	B.Sc. University of Sydney

Macquarie Island Party

Name	Age	Position	Qualifications
George Ainsworth	33	Leader Meteorologist	Services loaned from Commonwealth Meteorological Bureau
Leslie Blake	21	Geologist & Cartographer	
Harold Hamilton	26	Biologist	B.Sc Otago University
Charles Sandell	25	Wireless Operator & Mechanic	
Arthur Sawyer	26	Wireless Operator	

Senior Officers of the Aurora

Captain John King Davis Age 28	Captain of *Aurora* Master Mariner, previously Chief Officer and later Master of Nimrod on Shackleton's Expedition
Norman Toutcher	Chief Officer - July 1911-March 1912
Frank Fletcher	Chief Officer – April 1-12- March 1913
John Blair	Chief Officer – From September 1913
Percy Gray	Second Officer & Navigator
Clarence De La Motte	Third Officer
Frederick Gillies	Chief Engineer

Shaded Rows: Members of the Relief Party who remained for the second year.
* Published diary available

BANZARE: 1929-30 / 1930-31

BANZARE: Scientists		
Sir Douglas Mawson	Leader	
Professor T Harvey Johnson	Biologist	
Dr W Ingram	Medical Officer	
Harold Fletcher	Zoologist	
R G Simmers	Meteorologist	
Robert Falla	Ornithologist	
A Howard	Hydrologist	
JWS Marr	Hydrologist	
Commander Morton Moyes	Cartographer / Surveyor	Voyage 1
Alexander L Kennedy	Scientist	Voyage 2
Lieutenant C Oom	Cartographer	Voyage 2
Flight Lieutenant S Campbell	Aviator	
Pilot Officer E DouglasAviator		
Frank Hurley	Photographer	

BANZARE: *Officers of the Discovery*

John King Davis	Ship's Master Second in Command	Voyage 1
K N Mackenzie	First Officer	Voyage 1
	Ship's Master & Second in Command	Voyage 2
W R Colbeck	Second Officer	
J B Child	Third Officer	
W G Griggs	Chief Engineer	
Max Stanton	First Officer	Voyage 2

Shaded rows: Veterans of the AAE.

The Mawson's Huts Foundation

The Mawson's Huts Foundation was established as a not for profit charity in 1997 expressly to conserve the historic huts at Cape Denison, East Antarctica, used by the 1911-14 Australasian Antarctic Expedition (AAE) as its main base for two years.

Named after the AAE's leader, geologist and explorer Sir Douglas Mawson, the fragile wooden buildings are now known as known as "Mawson's Huts". They are rare as one of just six surviving sites of the "heroic era" of Antarctic exploration.

Situated 2730 kms directly south of Hobart, Tasmania, the historic buildings are regarded as the birthplace of Australia's Antarctic history. They also sit at what is officially the windiest place on earth at sea level where gusts up to 350 kph have been recorded. The average daily wind strength is just over 80 kph.

Between 1997 and 2015 the Foundation has organised and financed 11 major expeditions to the site with further planned for ongoing conservation and maintenance.

To assist with funding the expeditions the Foundation has built a full scale replica of the huts on the Hobart waterfront, just 200 metres from where Mawson departed in December 1911.

David Jensen, Chairman & CEO
Mawson's Huts Foundation
GPO Box 290
North Sydney
NSW 2088

WWW.Mawsons-huts.org.au
info@mawsons-huts.org.au

From top: Building the hut – January 1912
                Topping out – 2006
                The new roof – 2007

(The two bottom pictures © Mawson's Hut Foundation)

Ninnis as a Royal Fusilier

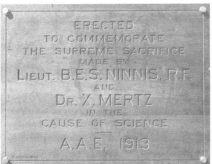

The memorial cross built by
Bickerton and raised by him and
McLean in 1913.

The plaque made by Hodgeman,
located at the foot of the cross.

Xavier Mertz

Karyn Maguire Bradford was born in Sydney, Australia. She studied History and Psychology at the University of Sydney, planning to become a History teacher but an oversupply of teaching graduates that year led her to seek opportunities elsewhere. In a radical career move she applied to train as an Air Traffic Controller, and joined a small group at the forefront of the entry of women into the profession. Karyn worked as a radar controller at Sydney airport for fifteen years before moving into the private sector and is currently the Logistics Coordinator for the Australian branch of a global manufacturing company.

She shares her house in Sydney with her husband, an ambassador from the tribe of Mrs Chippy, and a vast and growing pile of books, many of them related to her passionate interest in polar exploration. In 1995 she saw Antarctica from the air and hopes to actually set foot on the White Continent one day. This is her first published work.

Become a

Oscar Patrus

Dedication

This book is dedicated to everyone who said "I would not make it in the modelling industry" or that I should get a 'real job'.

I currently make over £250,000 a year in my 'real job' as one of the UK's most successful model coaches alongside the £100,000 I make from modelling, and more importantly, I've travelled the world and can honestly say the doubt you had in me led to my success.

THANKS, GUYS

Contents

CHAPTER 1

The truth about modelling

Thanks for buying my book. The aim of this book is to help you break into the modelling industry and make yourself a success.

I want to start by telling you these important truth's about modelling:

- I CANNOT make you a model.

- An agency or casting director CANNOT make you a model.

You will need to make yourself a model.

Despite what people think, it's not that hard to become a model. In fact, it's one of the easiest industries to break into.

Why? Because despite what most people believe:

- You do not need experience.

- You do not need to be super thin.

- You do not need to have abs of steel.

What you do need is drive and determination and a plan.

YOU WILL ALSO NEED to work hard to crack this industry. However, if you take the advice in this book, you can get signed to an agency and/or get freelancing jobs.

And when you do you will know that the only person you have to thank is YOU!

In my career, I've seen and worked with every type of model imaginable, including:

- Young, skinny, male and female

- Plus-size models

- Fitness models

- Sixty-nine-year-old ladies who want to "give it a go"

- Middle-aged men and women who want to reinvent themselves

- Child models

- Transsexual models

- Even ladies with beards.

All of the above can get modelling jobs. The key is knowing how to market yourself and having the drive to get out there and make it happen.

This book will explain the dos and don'ts so that when you do your first interview, casting, or job you are fully prepared.

So without further ado let's get started on making you a model . . .

How do we do that? We start with the basic questions that you need to answer yes to in order to succeed.

Question 1

ARE YOU COMMITTED?

If the answer is YES then ask yourself

HOW COMMITTED ARE YOU?

The answer should be 120%

If your answered matched mine then you are ready to start your modelling journey just remember wanting something and being committing to getting something are different things.

Think about it like this

You may want to win the lottery, but have you purchased a ticket?

Without one you CAN'T win.

The same applies to success in modelling

Question 2

Why do you want to be a model?

Write your answers here and keep it short:

_____

_____

_____

_____

_____

_____

In my experience of dealing with over 10,000 models, the common reasons why people decide to become models are closely linked to the following three things:

- Fame
- Money
- Lifestyle.

Any one of the above three answers is great. However, it is even better if you choose two or all of them.

CHAPTER 2

Becoming a model

There are four ways to start modelling:

1. Apply to modelling agencies (Page)

2. Get yourself some freelance jobs (Page)

3. Get scouted by a modelling agency (hardly ever happens)

4. Apply to modelling platforms (Page).

All of these methods are tried and tested and do work.

Any one of them could help you succeed in the industry.

However, in my experience, the best is a combination of two or more.

❖

CHAPTER 3

Why take my advice ?

So now we understand why you want to be a model and the paths you can use to get there i'd like to give you a little bit of my background and what got me into modelling.

When I was 17 I had braces and chunky glasses and was a little bit geeky; However, I had always wanted to be a model and to travel, appear in magazines, and have lots of money.

So, when I started applying to agencies my mum said I was crazy, my peers at school said I was too ugly, and the first agency I went to said I would never make it as I was too short.

Well, here I am 36 years later with over 2,000 modelling shoots under my belt. I've travelled most of the world and made a lot of money in my modelling career.

By the end of this book, I'm hoping you will know enough about the modelling industry to be able to fulfill your dream of being a model.

❖

CHAPTER 4

Mission Statement

Most models have a mission statement and I believe that in order to succeed in the industry you will also need one.

The purpose of a mission statement in modelling is to help keep you grounded and focused throughout your journey of breaking into the modelling industry.

To succeed in becoming a model you need to discover the type of model you are and how much time and effort you want to invest in modelling. You will also need to work hard and create yourself a brand that people want to buy. Your mission statement will help you to create that brand and define what it stands for.

Mission statements work for every kind of model, no matter if you are:

- A parent of a child model

- A 60-year-old lady

- A dashing young man

- A plus-size model
- Or Kate Moss.

To create your mission statement you will need to know the following:

- Where do you want to end up?
- How are you going to get there?
- What are you willing and not willing to do to get there?
- How committed are you?
- What will make you happy?

A great quote by Dave Ramsey that I kept in mind when creating my modelling mission statement is,

"Without a mission statement, you may get to the top of the ladder and then realise it was leaning against the wrong building!"

HERE IS A COPY OF MY MISSION STATEMENT

FOR MODELLING.

"My mission is to be a successful model who gets regular modelling jobs working in high-street and commercial fashion. I want to undertake eight to twelve modelling jobs a month and earn no less than £5,000 a month from my modelling jobs and £3,000 from my model coaching business. (www.themodel-coach.online)

It is important to me that I do modelling that fits with my career goals and to work with ethically mindful brands.

I will always act professionally on set and make sure I build strong relationships with my agent's and with members of the crew/production team when on set.

It is important to me that I have a good online reputation and that I use social media to promote myself in a positive light. I will not post or like controversial comments that could upset or hurt other people or my reputation.

I will make sure that I only coach models who can succeed. I will make sure that I genuinely help them to succeed, passing on the knowledge that I have learned throughout my modelling career.

I will dedicate five hours a week to self-development and progressing my career or learning more about the modelling industry and will make two new industry contacts every week."

*** *Spend at least one week writing your mission statement look at it everyday and see how you can improve it.*

❖

CHAPTER 5

Do you have the looks to become a model?

First and foremost, there is no set standard or size you need to be in order for you to be a model. The only restrictions on you being a model are your drive, determination, and personality.

In my experience when people ask me this question they normally mean, 'Am I pretty enough?', 'What about my height?', 'Have I got the right measurements?'.

My answer is and has always been, '**YES.** You have what it takes to be a model and your body shape or face has little to do with whether YOU CAN be a model and more to do with WHAT TYPE of model you can be.

Being aware of your measurements ensures you attend castings relevant to your body type. Determining your body measurements may seem difficult, especially for new models. I have put together some simple guidelines to follow in order to help you accurately find your measurements and identify your body type.

❖

CHAPTER 6

Measuring your body for modelling

Agencies and clients will immediately be able to tell if you provide incorrect measurements. Handing over wrong measurements looks unprofessional and can negatively affect your chances of being hired by these agencies and clients.

Generally, there are three basic measurements in determining body shape: bust, waist, and hips. However, it is becoming more common to also know your shoulder measurements. Knowing this number on the off-chance that it may be required by an agency or client will make you look well-prepared and professional.

For women, depending on who you ask, some say it's best to wear a bra while taking your measurements, while others disagree. If you decide to wear a bra, make sure it's one that doesn't contain padding or any other enhancing elements. Determining your body shape means measuring how your body naturally is.

*** TIP: Measuring your body requires a flexible body-measuring tape. It's recommended to wear tight yet comfortable clothing; this prevents extra clothing fabric from affecting the accuracy of your measurements.*

SHOULDERS

To measure your shoulders, keep your back straight and shoulders relaxed. Extend the tape measure from the outer edge of one shoulder to the outer edge of the other. In doing so, keep the tape measure parallel to the floor. To find out your measurement, simply turn your head to the side and read the tape measure without altering your posture.

BUST

Begin by wrapping the tape measure around your back and across the centre of your bust. Be sure to measure the fullest part of your bust all the way around in order to obtain an accurate number. The point where one end of the tape meets the other on the front of your chest is your bust measurement.

WAIST

Measuring your waist requires wrapping the tape measure around the smallest part of your waistline. This area is known as the natural waist. To avoid confusion of where this particular point is, it's useful to note that your natural waist is above your belly button and just below your rib cage. Run your hands along the sides of your body to identify where your rib cage ends. Start from the back with your tape measure and bring it to the centre of your front to find your measurement. Though it may be tempting, I urge you to avoid sucking in or holding your breath. Keep your stomach relaxed and be sure not to pull the tape measure too tight.

Hips

When finding the measurement of your hips, begin with your feet close together. Next, start from the back and wrap the measuring tape around the fullest part of your bum, and continue with it going around the widest area of your hips – this is typically where your hip bones are located. To do this accurately, make sure the tape measure is parallel to the floor.

CHAPTER 7

Body Shape

Identifying your overall body-shape type isn't always straightforward, even after taking your measurements. The following are rough guidelines for determining which shape your body is.

INVERTED TRIANGLE:

- Wide shoulders
- Narrow hips

TRIANGLE/PEAR:

- Narrow shoulders
- Proportionately wide waist and hips

HOURGLASS:

- Proportionate shoulders and hips
- Narrow waist

FIGURE-8:

- Proportioned hips and shoulders

- Rounded tummy

- Proportionate weight distribution

OVAL/APPLE:

- Narrow shoulders

- Skinny legs

- Rounded stomach

***Tip – Go to a high-street store or tailor such as John Lewis or Selfridges they will normally measure you for free.

CHAPTER 8

Types of modelling based on measurements

I have compiled an outline of what measurements different types of modelling require. However, every designer, brand, and country differs. Speak to your agency to find out more about which modelling sector your body is best suited for.

RUNWAY/CATWALK

Female

Height: 5'9–6'0"
Bust: 32–34"
Waist: 23–35"

Male

Height: 6'0" minimum
Waist: 31–33"

COMMERCIAL (PRINT)
Female

Height: 5'7–6'0"
Bust: 32–34"
Waist: 23–25"
Hips: 33–35"

Male

A thin, tall body type

COMMERCIALS
Female

Height: No minimum height requirements
Waist/Hips: Dress size 6–8 (sometimes extending to 10)

Male

Height: No minimum height requirements
Waist: 31–35"

EDITORIAL
Female

Height: 5'8–6'0"
Bust: 32–34"
Waist: 23–25"
Hips: 33–35"

Male

Height: 6'0" minimum
Waist: 31–33"

PLUS-SIZE

Height: 5'8" minimum
Size: 14–20, depending on the market

❖

CHAPTER 9

Know your strengths

At the very beginning of your modelling career, I recommend taking the time to identify your strengths. Recognise which of your features are best and most unique. Ultimately, understand what traits will set you apart from the competition.

After identifying your strongest attributes, it's important to research which agencies and brands could be the best fit for your individual look. This also gives you an idea of where you fit in the fashion and modelling industry. As a result you'll be able to show agencies and clients that you're right for the job when attending castings. Knowing the areas in which you excel will make it so much easier to get signed and start working.

STRENGTHS OF A SUCCESSFUL MODELS

- Ability to POSE
- The model should take direction well
- Have an adaptable image
- be able to visually connect with the camera

❖

CHAPTER 10

Types of modelling

COMMERCIAL

In commercial modelling, models are hired to promote products and services through advertisements. Brands such as Boots or Superdrug use models to reach consumers through media like billboards, magazines, and TV advertisements.

As commercial models must be relatable in order to sell products, model requirements (such as age, height, size) vary depending on the company. In this modelling sector, individuals can make anything between £800–£10,000 per job. (as a rule of thumb its the lower end of this amount, however i do have a friend who recently got £8000 for a toothpaste advert which she worked on for 2 days and she is an average everyday model).

HIGH-STREET FASHION

According to one of the UK's leading modelling platforms, GT Models, high-street fashion modelling is the most sought-after area of work by new models from the 70,000 applicants they get a year.

High-street fashion refers to the type of clothing that is readily available and can be purchased from shops in your town or city centre.

Modelling for Zara, Topshop, and H&M are the types of brands you would work with as a high street fashion model. These brands need models for campaigns for two distinct seasons – autumn and winter (AW) and spring and summer (SS). However, in between these main seasons, brands also produce garments that are similar to the items already available for that season but that may differ slightly, for example in neckline or pattern. The images produced are used for posters in shop windows or ads on the company's website.

Working for high-street fashion brands is best accomplished with an agency's help. Your agent will

- Set up model castings for you to attend

- When hired, they will correspond with the company to discuss your payment rate

- Confirm when the shoot will be (date and time), where the shoot will take place, and approximately how many hours the shoot will last.

In terms of high-street fashion modelling, many models are able to find consistent and well-paid, full-time work. While hourly rates vary greatly depending on your experience, models are able to earn up to £1,000 per shoot.

If a job is booked through your agency, a fee of 20 per cent will be deducted from the job's total earnings. For example, a model will take home £800 from a shoot paying £1,000. Travel costs may also be covered by the company. This is something that should be discussed with your agency BEFORE accepting the job.

TV AND FILM

Individuals who pursue TV and film may do so as a way to establish themselves as an actor or simply to gain more industry experience in front of the camera. TV and film modelling includes jobs like being an extra in a regional soap opera or being part of a toothpaste advertisement. Depending on the job, TV and film models can make anywhere between £300–£500.

HIGH FASHION

High fashion, not to be confused with high-street fashion, tends to be the top end of the market. As a rule, you need to be super-thin and very tall (around 5'9" or above). Although high-fashion modelling can pay very well, it is one of the hardest areas of the industry to break into due to a strict set of physical requirements.

FITNESS

To do this you need to be super-dedicated and be willing to work out a lot and stay at your prime fitness. There tend not to be as many fitness modelling jobs as high-fashion or general commercial jobs available, but there is also a lot less competition, as not so many people have the willpower to maintain that sort of fitness.

LINGERIE

Generally speaking, clients look for female models with a pretty face, curvy figure, and natural breasts. Desirable physiques for male models are roughly lean without being overly muscular. More specifically, clients desire female models with slim and slender physiques. For women, a toned stomach is a must. Men are required to achieve a polished six-pack to complement their toned arms and legs. For the most part, lingerie designers or brands don't hire models that have a physique that's too skinny or athletic. Again, this comes down to the desire for individuals who correctly fill out the designs.

***Tip – Once you work in lingerie modelling it can be hard to get castings in other types of modelling, as it carries a stigma.

PLUS-SIZE

What many aspiring plus-size models do not realise is that the body type for this modelling sector is specific. Just because a model is labeled 'plus-size' does not mean that they can be unhealthy, overweight, or out of shape. In other words, plus-size models are a fit and healthy representation of the everyday person. To work in this sector, models must be at least 5'8" and a

UK size 12–16.

Just like those working in other modelling sectors, plus-size models must possess ample confidence and have an outgoing personality. Confidence paired with a positive attitude is a great way to stand out with agencies and clients. It shows them that you are open to challenges and feel comfortable working in front of the camera.

CATALOGUE MODELLING

Catalogue modelling involves posing for clothing and product catalogues and is needed for both print and online campaigns. A high number of models find success in this sector as the requirements for models depend on the specific brand. One brand may cater to a certain body type and age while the target customer of another brand differs completely.

The range of catalogue modelling jobs is extensive. Brands like Mamas and Papas, John Lewis and Missguided use print and online catalogues to reach audiences. For the fashion industry's two main seasons, AW and SS, brands require models for their print and digital catalogues. As a catalogue model, an individual must have a relatable look in order to reach large audiences. Additionally, it's typical for brands to hire models who have healthy hair, glowing skin, and nice teeth. However, the desired look all comes down to the brand's individual identity and style.

CHILD MODELLING

Due to the importance and complexity of child modelling, there are separate guidelines on this. Please see Section 12 of this book.

❖

CHAPTER 11

Applying to agencies

Before I tell you how to apply to an agency, I want to explain what an agency is . . .

Simply put, a modelling agency is a business that rents out products, like a library or a car rental company. They have a group of models, and they take these models and try to rent them out to other companies.

Many new models think that modelling agencies decide who gets a job. They don't think of it this way, for example:

- A fizzy drinks company (Green Cola) want to put out a summer advert for Diet Green Cola. They contact an agency; let's call this agency Magpie Models.

- Green Cola send the job to Magpie Models stating that they are looking for three models two teenagers and someone to play the mother.

- Magpie Models then send Green Cola the portfolios or Z-cards of their models who fit the criteria.

- Green Cola then choose which models they want to meet . . . and who gets the job. . .

So, the important thing to take from this example is this: if you don't get a job, don't blame your agency. Remember, they want you to get as many jobs as possible, as the more jobs you do, the more commission they make.

They will try to get you as many jobs as possible. However, they have NO control over whether or not you get the job.

❖

CHAPTER 12

Before you apply – prepare yourself

Now you understand how a modelling agency works, you need to start applying to them. Normally, your agency will ask for simple images before they decide if they want to meet you. These are normally basic images with no filters on them and no makeup on your skin or if you are an established model with a full portfolio you should send this.

When you apply, you should not do it on impulse – prepare in advance. Here is a list of things to do BEFORE YOU APPLY to your chosen agencies:

1. Make sure you fit the agency's criteria. Don't waste their time or yours.

2. Write your introductory statement/letter(Page 55)

3. Make a list of any questions you want to ask the agency.

4. Have some plain photos ready with no makeup or filters on them.

5. Have your diary to hand in case they want to book an appointment with you.

6. Have your portfolio prepared and up to date.

7. Use a professional email, for example Jane-Model@ gmail.com, not Silly Sally!£@hotmail.com.

Most models don't think these things are important, and maybe for the the model they most likely not important. However, having spoken to over 200 model bookers, I can assure you that, for the agency or platform they are.

Here are some questions agencies will ask themselves when looking at your application:

- Does this person present themselves as a professional model?

- Do I believe they will be committed?

- Can I get them work?

- If I get them work, will they reflect well on my agency?

How you act when applying to the agency will 100% determine what the agency thinks of you as a person and, therefore, will likely determine whether or not they are willing to sign you and start looking for modelling jobs for you.

POTENTIAL TO SIGN

If the agency likes your application, you will most likely be invited to their office for a face-to-face meeting. If models are under the age of 18 a reputable agency will insist on meeting a biological parent or legal guardian. They will normally want documentation to prove their identity.

***Tip – A legal guardian is not a friend of the family or a family member. Check with the agency before you bring anyone other than a parent, as if you get it wrong they will send you away and not invite you back.

Following this meeting, the agency will decide whether you are what they want and whether they can get you any work. If all goes well, they will offer you a contract, as everything needs to be agreed in writing.

***Tip - A good agency will insist on having everything documented. That way there is never any confusion over pay, jobs, contracts, what the offer entails, etc.

The contracts agencies offer are normally standard and the same for all models in that category. For example, a catwalk model may have 20%t of their earnings taken, whereas a TV extra may have 15% taken. However, this is always covered in the early stages of the contract being offered and, as a rule of thumb, is not up for negotiation.

The important thing when signing a contract, in my opinion, is that you ensure you have the option to say no to jobs you don't want and that you are ideally on an non-exclusive contract, meaning that you CAN be signed and working with other companies and agencies.

Following the agreement of all of the above, the agency will normally take some Polaroid photos and a copy of your Z-cards or digital portfolio. Once the contract is signed and they have your portfolio, industry experts working at the agency can assess the models and their photos in the hope of getting them their first paid modelling job. The sooner that happens, the sooner the model makes money, and the sooner the agency make commission.

Agency Loyalty

Some models make an agreement with their new agency that they will not approach rival agencies. However, their contracts are not a lifelong commitment, and they are given the freedom to change agencies once their career develops. With that said, it's common for younger models to stay with their original agencies for long periods of time. If signed at a young age, such as 16, models develop a close professional relationship with their agencies.

Finding Work

Modelling agencies send new models to castings, giving them the opportunity to find work. This is a chance for models to meet other creatives, like fashion brand representatives or photographers, working in the industry. If a model lives outside the city where their agency is based, it's common practice for agencies to keep a 'model flat' where multiple models are able to stay for a few nights. This allows them time to attend numerous casting calls and gives them the opportunity to network with other individuals in the industry.

AFTERCARE

Whether models have found success or are still gaining positive exposure, modelling agencies must continue caring for their models. models may contact an agency to inform them of new casting appointments. It's also important for agencies and models to work together to keep a model's portfolio up to date. To be a successful model or a successful agency, communication is crucial. When both sides remain committed and passionate about their roles, their ability to flourish in the fashion and modelling industry is strengthened.

To summarise, there is an agency for everyone. Some of the best agencies out there specialise in models that are not 'typical model material'. Don't be disheartened if you don't get signed by the first agency you apply to its quite normal to get knock-backs in the early days.

❖

CHAPTER 13

Alternative agencies

Here, I've put together four of my favourite agencies to show that, despite what most people think, there really are modelling opportunities for everyone, providing you are willing to find them.

UGLY MODELS AGENCY WWW.UGLY.ORG

Ugly Models Agency represents models and actors varying drastically in age, height, size, and look. To quote its website – 'We like our women fat and our men geeky, we like the extremely tall and the shockingly small. "If you're a model with a unique appearance and a vibrant personality, Ugly Models is a fantastic agency to contact. Even with their long list of dynamic characters, Ugly Models also represents individuals with a more traditional look".

ANTI-AGENCY WWW.ANTIAGENCY.CO.UK

Anti-Agency revolves around selecting models with endless individual style and personality. Many clients represented by Anti-Agency pursue other areas of the creative industry, like music and art. Models whose personalities rival their colourful appearances are the perfect fit. Clients like Marc Jacobs and Dazed & Confused turn to Anti-Agency to find models possessing a strong individual style and a charismatic personality to effectively represent their brands.

TMA Models https://www. tmatalentmanagement.co.uk/

TMA Talent Management is extremely selective with the clients they take onto there books and will only take on those they honestly feel have a good chance of getting work, whether this is for modelling, acting or supporting artist (SA/extra) work. When TMA Models' books are open, each individual application is carefully assessed and successful applicants are contacted within five working days to arrange a face-to-face meeting.

Apple Model Management www. applemodels.com

From a quick look on Apple Model Management's website it may not appear dramatically different to other traditional modelling agencies. However, this Thailand-based agency caters to a modelling category that has gained popularity throughout the fashion industry in recent years. Aside from signing models fit for the runway and high-fashion editorials, Apple Model Management also prides itself on representing some of the industry's most talented transgender models.

Milk Models www.milkmanagement.co.uk

Milk Models "ethos is that no two models are alike and thus tailor their approach to suit each individual to foster growth across all boards. Having discovered some significant players in the modelling and talent arena, MiLK has grown in notoriety in its 6 years since inception. Forming the pillar of success for the agency is MiLK's team of Agents." which i just think it a great way for an agency to look at the industry. Also take a look at the influencer page on there site to see some truly inspiring models

http://www.milkmanagement.co.uk/search/portfolio/Influencers

Norrie Carr Models http://www.norriecarr.com/

The above agencies are just a few that prove that success in the fashion industry isn't solely reserved for classic beauties or those meeting traditional requirements. No matter who you are, there's an agency suited to your individual look

Model Platforms

A modelling platform is a new concept that has been around for the last 10-15 years the great thing about the platform is the scale of them they are normally equipped to handle many more models than an agency and have access to big databases of modelling agencies

When you start modelling you don't know who to contact, who is good, which agencies have there books open thats where platforms come in they do all of this for you and cut out lots of the leg work that a new model would normally need to do some of the best platforms in the UK and ireland are

- **Models Plus - www.modelsplus.com**

- **Assets Models Ireland www.assetsmodels.com**

- **UK Models www.ukmodels.co.uk**

- **GT Models www.gtmodel.co.uk**

❖

CHAPTER 14

Freelance Modelling

When first starting out modelling, many models opt for finding an agency to represent them. While agencies are fantastic in helping models gain their footing in the industry, some prefer the freelance route. Freelance modelling is the perfect option for people who wish to be their own boss and manage their career independently. The really clever models do both.

WHAT IS FREELANCE MODELLING?

Essentially, freelance modelling is when you represent yourself as a model instead of waiting for an agency to find you jobs. As a freelance model, it is your responsibility to find work, market yourself, build your portfolio, and network throughout the industry. Working as a freelance model means devoting as much time as you see fit to your career. Freelance models have the freedom to seek full- or part-time work, depending on their schedule.

ADVANTAGES OF FREELANCE MODEL?

Perhaps one of the most desirable features of freelance modelling is the fact that models take home the entire amount of money they earn from modelling jobs. As you are representing yourself, there is no need to pay agency fees. Additionally, as freelance models aren't represented by an agency, there is no need to fit any standard requirements with regards to physical appearance, as can be demanded by agencies. However, this does not mean neglecting a healthy lifestyle and regular exercise regime. All models in the industry, no matter which sector or type of representation they fall under, must follow nutritious eating habits paired with weekly workouts.

***Tip – Before looking for freelance jobs, read my 'staying safe' (page 55).

FINDING FREELANCE WORK

Typically, freelance models find more success, at least at the beginning of their career, with local photographers and companies.

Many models use websites like www.ModelMayhem.com or www.starnow.com

Spend a minimum of 5 hours a week conducting thorough online research about available modelling jobs is one of the best ways a freelance model can find work as you can arrange your portfolio to fit the needs of the client.

Freelance models also have the option of signing non-exclusive agency contracts. A great number of non-exclusive-contract models undertake freelance work alongside their agency work, meaning they have a higher chance of securing work.

Types of freelance modelling jobs

As a freelance model, there is no restrictions on the types of work you can choose to take. Print, commercial, promo, catalogue, and fitness modelling are just a few types of work individuals can choose from. In the modelling industry, the demand for models is extremely high. From magazine ads for fashion brands to pamphlets discussing flu jabs distributed by the NHS, models are in constant demand. With that said, fashion brands typically contact agencies when seeking models for editorials and runway shows.

Freelance rates

The rates for freelance modelling jobs differ from individual to individual. Before booking a job, it's common practice for companies to disclose a set rate for that particular job. This rate greatly depends on the brand, the model's experience, the model's portfolio, and the number of hours required by a specific job. Generally, hourly rates for models (both freelance and signed) can range from £40 to over £1,000.

Furthermore, adult models make higher rates than children and teen models, due to the legal restrictions placed on the working hours of younger models.

UNPAID WORK

Remember, it's extremely common practice for any model starting out in the industry, no matter their representation, to take unpaid work. Although obtaining paid jobs is every model's dream, unpaid work helps individuals build their portfolios, gain valuable experience, network with others in the industry, and increase their exposure.

While this can mean dedicating many hours of your time and energy without payment the experience can be its own reward just as an athlete trains for an event you can train for modelling . Furthermore, working for free gives models the opportunity to gain modelling experience and meet a variety of creatives working in the fashion industry.

*** *Tip - Think of it as training or being an apprentice, at the end it's all practise and "practise makes perfect"*

❖

CHAPTER 15

K nowing how to act on a shoot is just as important as how good you are in front of the camera, make a good impression you could get more work make a bad impression and get a bad reputation.

ACCEPTING YOUR FIRST JOB

As a model, no two days are the same. One week you may be hired for a chic catalogue shoot in a top London studio and the next you're posing alongside exotic animals in a location miles away from home. Between photographers, clients, stylists, make-up artists, and set designers, a model's 'little black book' holds the capacity to grow exponentially. With a growing network of contacts and increased photoshoot experience, a model's chances of undertaking exciting, innovative work immediately open up. With that in mind, there are guidelines to follow when it comes to accepting modelling jobs.

STEPPING OUTSIDE OF YOUR COMFORT ZONE

Doing something for the first time can be extremely scary, especially if there's a whole crew of photographers, make-up artists and stylists watching. Perhaps a photographer asks you to pose while on a horse (and you've never ridden one before) or jump into a pool (and you don't know how to swim) – instances like this may force models out of their comfort zones during photo shoots. Posing in unexpected ways, utilising unconventional props, or wearing unique garments are everyday occurrences faced by models. It's okay for a task to seem daunting. In fact, embrace that feeling! Overcoming some fears to effectively showcase your talents and capture a beautiful end result is what modelling is all about.

OUTSIDE YOUR COMFORT ZONE DOESN'T MEAN BEING UNCOMFORTABLE

Particularly if you are new to modelling, certain tasks or photo shoots are going to appear intimidating; it's completely natural. To grow as a model and expand your industry knowledge, give every job your best – ask questions, experiment, and have fun! It should be noted, however, that stepping outside of your comfort zone completely differs from doing things you are personally and morally uncomfortable with. If you are ever offered a modelling job and you feel it is not a good fit for you, turn it down. You should never feel pressured to accept jobs that go against any of your personal beliefs.

*** *Tip – Before saying yes to a job, speak with your agent to find out more information so that you understand what the job entails.*

NEVER SAY YES TO A JOB AND THEN DON'T TURN UP

Although it's entirely acceptable for a model to turn down a job he or she feels is not a good fit, failing to turn up for a job after agreeing to do it, even not turning up for casting or interview can get you blacklisted.

After accepting a job, if you do not show up, it communicates to clients that you are unprofessional and lack commitment in the modelling industry. As reputation speaks volumes in this line of work, failing to show up to a job can negatively impact how others perceive you and can make it difficult to find future employment. Not attending a job is disrespectful to everyone involved and costs the client a great deal of time, energy, and money.

I always find the easiest way to explain this is with an example, so then I can also reiterate the importance of making sure that, if you take a job, you turn up with that in mind. I'm going to tell you about a conversation I had recently with an owner of one of TMA Model Company's models.

They had a young model around the age of 17. For the sake of the example, let's call him Tommy.

Tommy was offered a job for a large UK brand. It was a one-day shoot in London, and he was going to be paid £15,000. The agency would have taken 20 per cent, so Tommy would end up with £12,000 for one day's work.

The amount paid was decided by the brand. How it works is that the brand advertises the job, the agency sends the model for a casting or sends their portfolio, the model gets chosen, and the fee is always decided before the job is offered.

However, things did not go according to plan. Tommy accepted the job, and the night before the shoot the agency spoke to him and confirmed he was going.

On the day of the shoot, the company arranging it rang the agency, as Tommy didn't turn up for the job. When they spoke to him on the phone, he said, 'My friends talked me out of it, so I went to Cardiff for a few days'. Tommy got dropped from his agency!

The company paying for the shoot still had to pay for the photographer, makeup artist, set hire, set design, etc. It ended up costing £10,000 for the shoot and not one image was taken!

Moral of the story:

IF YOU SAY YES TO A JOB, YOU MAKE SURE YOU TURN UP!

QUESTIONS TO ASK YOUR PHOTOGRAPHER

Prior to arriving at a photo shoot, a model's agent, or the model if working freelance, should have open communication with photographers to ensure a successful shoot. Taking the proper steps and conducting adequate research before attending a modelling job will make the day run more smoothly and help establish a professional working environment.

- what should you bring to the shoot

- details of the mood of the shoot

- expectations from you as a model

- will they be providing direction

- what research would they recommend you taking prior to arriving at the shoot

- do they have a mood/concept board or sketches for the shoot

KNOW YOUR PHOTOGRAPHER

When you're signed to an agency, it's your agent's job to know the client booking you and who will be working as the photographer. If you work as a freelance model, then it's up to you to conduct your own research into who you will be working with. Before saying yes to a job, do some research. Have a look at the photographer's portfolio to get a feel for their shooting style and what types of work they have done previously. This will give you a better understanding of whether or not the proposed job is something that fits you and that you're comfortable with.

SHOOT DETAILS

Knowing the date, time, and location of a photo shoot before it takes place may seem like common sense. However, it's not always as straightforward as it sounds. A photo shoot requires the assistance of many creatives, such as stylists, photographers, models, make-up artists, and set designers. Scheduling a time that works for all involved, especially if done by those working freelance, may mean rescheduling the shoot multiple times. Be sure to have all of the shoot's up-to-date details prior to arriving to avoid keeping anyone waiting. Furthermore, ensure that you understand how to get there. Showing up late wastes time and money and reflects poorly in terms of industry professionalism.

***Tip – Double confirm with your agent all the details via **EMAIL NOT PHONE** *the day before the shoot.*

PAYMENT

Discussing payment is something your modelling agency will do with the client before offering you the job. Working freelance will require models to speak with those involved in order to reach an agreed-upon amount. If the job is unpaid, this should be clearly established before making a decision about whether or not you wish to do the job.

*** Tip – Once a fee is agreed, do NOT try to negotiate for more money.

Shoot Expectations

I can't stress enough the importance of knowing what to expect from a shoot before agreeing to do it. Speak with your photographer about the shoot themes, outfits, desired poses, etc. This helps avoid the chances of feeling uncomfortable and unsafe at a photoshoot. Agreeing to a shoot where you do not feel comfortable working will affect your confidence and performance, and ultimately the outcome of the images. As a model, remember that you do not have to abstain from your values and beliefs. Always put your safety and standards first in terms of accepting a job.

Model Release Form

Understanding the meaning of a model release form is vital when entering the industry. These forms give legal permission for a model's photographs to be used by photographers. It is highly encouraged for all models and photographers to sign this prior to shooting. Model release forms prohibit photographers from using your images without your consent.

❖

CHAPTER 16

Travelling for modelling jobs

Working in the modelling industry, you may be asked to travel for certain jobs. Many times, where you travel to depends on your specific look and what type of market different locations cater to, as beauty standards differ all around the world. Having been in the industry for so many years, I believe the best part of the industry is the travelling. Not only does it generally pay the best money, it's great life experience too.

TRAVEL JOBS - GETTING THEM

Finding proper representation with reputable modelling agencies is the best way to land travelling jobs. Without agency backing, it can be extremely difficult for models to find work in other locations. Having an agency makes it easier as they will get in touch with the appropriate contacts and ask all the necessary questions.

Additionally, modelling agents know the fashion industry like the back of their hand. They will be able to determine which market you are best suited for.

For example, in South Africa clients tend to look for models with tan skin, while in Tokyo young models with fair skin and fresh faces are often sought after.

Doing your research and only working with an established agency ensures you do not make the mistake of travelling to a market not suited to you and finding no work. i always advise the models in my model coaching company to remember that even with correct representation, finding travelling jobs as a model still requires a great deal of perseverance, patience, market knowledge, and strong connections.

AGENCY CONNECTIONS

For models with agency representation, your agents are the ones who will handle your placement. The main agency you're with is known as your mother agency. It is your base and located in the country you live in. Typically, mother agencies have sister agencies located in different countries. Much of the work in finding modelling jobs in other locations depends on your main agency. Your agent will normally submit you to a different agencies.

If they are interested in you and your look, it's common that you will be asked to make a video so they can see how you move and act. There's a good chance that all communication will stay between your mother agency and the agency you're travelling to.

Your main agency will help you attain all of the legal contracts and proper documents, like a visa, if needed. Many models already have a contract before travelling to their destination. Ensure your mother agency provides you with this information prior to accepting the job.

LENGTH OF PLACEMENT

The length of placement will differ for each modelling job. Between one and two weeks is the typical amount of time a short-term travelling contract lasts for a model in another market.

A long-term contract usually lasts between one and three months. An agreement contract specifies how long you will be gone, where you will go, what will be expected of you, your rates in regards to pay (if it is a paid opportunity), and any other specific details. While this is not always the case, a good agency will insist that all models under the age of 18 travel with a parent or guardian, especially if travelling to a different country.

ARRIVING IN YOUR NEW LOCATION

Arriving in a new city, especially one where a different language is spoken, can be extremely daunting and stressful. For this reason, speak to your mother agency before leaving and have them arrange for an individual from the new agency to meet you at the airport. At the very least, the new agency should send you the address to the flat where you will be staying before you arrive. After you get settled into your accommodation, it's important that your next step should be for you to go and see your new agent. During your meeting, they will take new photos of you and provide you with pocket money, a phone, and internet access.

TRAVEL EXPENSES

The amount of travel expenses covered during your travelling modelling job completely depends on the agency and/or client you're signed with. Typically, expenses, flights, accommodation, and any phone charges will all be deducted from your pay at the end of your contract.

Agencies can also typically take anywhere between 20% and 40% of your earnings. Following your stay, you will receive all of the money you made during your time, minus expenses and agency fees. Certain clients may cover **ALL** of your expenses if you travel for a specific job. However, do not expect this to be the case most of the time, particularly if you are a new model.

If you're a model who wishes to travel, it's your responsibility to determine just how far you're willing to go for a job. Identify the pros and cons of travelling to a different city, country, or continent. My recommendation is that if you are offered a travelling modelling job, embrace the opportunity. It's a great way to network, gain experience, and learn about other countries and cultures.

CHAPTER 17

Modelling and Social Media

The internet can be a powerful tool to use in order to gain exposure if used correctly or it could ruin your chances of success if used badly.

With the number of people and companies possessing an online presence, using social media appropriately is an effective and free way to grab attention. With that being said, I suggest creating separate social media accounts – a personal account and a professional account.

Many aspiring models forget that modelling is an occupation that and success relies on how people perceive you. Using your personal accounts, full of self-taken photos portraying the intimate details of your life, doesn't read well with potential clients. Unless you're already established, it's highly recommended to only include professionally taken photos (i.e. those from your modelling portfolio or modelling jobs) on your social media accounts.

Posting solely professional photographs lets potential clients and contacts know that you take your modelling career seriously and present yourself professionally.

Social media is fast becoming a platform that aspiring models use to kick-start their careers. While signing to a modelling agency, attending model castings, and working on professional photo shoots are the best ways to gain essential modelling experience.

WHICH PLATFORM?

With the number of social platforms out there, it may be difficult to decide which platform to use to represent yourself. Instagram, typically, is the first choice for many aspiring models due to its image-based nature. Other platforms, like Twitter and Facebook, are great for putting yourself out there and networking with a wider demographic. However it also allows you to show your opinion rather than just your looks if your images are what you want to show off, Instagram should definitely be your first choice.

CREATE YOUR BRAND

Before you start posting, understand how you want to present yourself. What is your reason for establishing yourself on Instagram? Furthermore, what type of modelling are you looking to break into? For example, you may choose to show off more of your body if your desire is to become a glamour model, if your desire is to model for high street fashion brands then post images similar to what high street fashion brands post on their websites.

***TIP - Do your research to see what models in your desired sector are doing on social media.

Once you know how you want to be seen, post photos and videos that capture that. Be sure to use the same filters in order to make your page cohesive, and don't go overboard with the amount. Try to limit yourself to always using one to two filters for the photos and videos you post. Additionally, consider the background environment. While you won't always be posting in the same place (for example, you may usually take photos from your home but want to upload some from the last trip you took), posting photos that have a similar theme also helps in maintaining a cohesive vibe.

*** Tip - Don't post pictures of yourself on a night out, smoking or with snapchat dog ears on your professional facebook page

KNOW YOUR AUDIENCE

In order to reach out to people and gain followers, it's vital to understand who you're targeting. Which demographic do you appeal to most? What are the ages and careers of those you want to reach? Are you trying to gain more male or female followers? These are all questions you should be asking yourself as you build your Instagram presence.

CONSISTENCY

Social media is all about consistency. It's difficult to engage others with what you're doing if you post sporadically. To maintain a consistent following, be sure to post multiple times a day. This will keep your content fresh and make others wonder what you're going to post next. It also shows your dedication to your followers and that you're committed to your brand.

Here are my top three ideas of how to expand your social media presence:

- Add or follow ten new industry-based professionals per week. This could include photographers, make-up artists, other models, fashion brands, stylists, and modelling agencies.

- Post positive comments/likes on other people's work.

- Spend a few hours making a list of high-ranking modelling related tags to use whenever you post.

CHOOSE WISELY

How you wish to portray yourself is completely up to you. At the end of the day, it is your Instagram account. However, if your dream is to become a commercial model for high-fashion brands, posting semi-nude images may not be the best choice.

Again, your Instagram account is meant to propel your career, not sabotage it. Use it as a way to express your unique personality in a way that goes hand in hand with the type of modelling you are aiming to gain success in.

In the modelling industry, gaining exposure and networking with other creatives is essential. Traditionally, this was done during castings or meetings with agencies. In today's world, however, social media has made it much easier to reach out and establish a voice of your own. If you're looking to excel in your modelling career, having a strong online presence on social media is a fantastic first step.

*** *Tip - Do your social media pages match your mission statement?*

TWITTER

Twitter is a great platform to instantly reach out and connect with others. With its 140-character messages, you can instantly share your opinion on the latest trends and fashion shows and contact any industry individuals, such as other models. Find your tone of voice and go with it. From witty to serious, find a tone of voice that best fits your personality. When posting media, for example photos, do your best to share striking content. As Twitter is predominantly text-based, any visual content should be eye-catching.

***Tip *— Be careful! It's easy to post your thoughts here, and what you say be misunderstood. I personally avoid Twitter. (if you must use it make sure you have a positive tone)*

FACEBOOK

Unlike other social media platforms, where glimpses into your personal life are welcome, models should be cautious when it comes to Facebook. Due to the fact that Facebook consists of many types of ways to share information, it's best to create separate accounts – one for your personal life and another one for your professional life. Separating the two makes sharing photos from family get-togethers or reaching out to contacts about shoot collaboration much easier. Creating a Facebook page solely for your career and those in your industry also looks more professional.

*** *Tip - Keep your private account PRIVATE*

LinkedIn

Considering LinkedIn was created for business professionals to network, naturally, it's a site you want to be active on. While the site isn't for posting anything personal or unprofessional, it's great for connecting with those in various industries. Models use LinkedIn for corresponding with make-up artists, photographers, potential clients, other models, etc. Additionally, individuals you connect with are able to see your experience and other professionals you've collaborated with.

When it comes to your personality and social media, don't be afraid to show it off! Including personal photos and information makes you relatable while also giving you a sense of uniqueness. With that said, although it's imperative to show off your personality and life, don't forget to keep it professional.

Lastly, consistency is key. Regular posting helps with continued exposure and increases the opportunity to network with more individuals in the industry. It shows that you're serious about selling your brand and are actively looking to expand your port-folio and grow your following.

Recommendations of who to follow on social media

https://www.instagram.com/vogue/?hl=en

https://www.instagram.com/models1/?hl=en

https://www.instagram.com/explore/tags/modelling/?hl=en

https://www.instagram.com/explore/tags/fashion-shoots/?hl=en

https://www.instagram.com/explore/tags/freelancemodel-ling/?hl=en

https://www.instagram.com/starnow/?hl=en

CHAPTER 18

❖

Portfolio

A portfolio is a model's greatest weapon in job-hunting. It is a collection of your best images and is what casting directors will use to decide on whether you are what they are looking for. In essence, it is your CV. When you first build a portfolio, it is important that you use professional images, as a collection of your best holiday photos is not going to cut it with anyone.

Your agency will advise you of the type of portfolio you are likely to need. As a catwalk model's portfolio will differ to that of a commercial model's, you need images that will get you noticed within your specific area.

In general, a set of diverse pictures showing you in a range of styles and locations with a varying range of shots will give you more chance of being cast due to showing that you are adaptable and that you can fit into the client's vision.

Once you have undertaken a number of shoots you can then add to your portfolio and use these new pictures to develop and extend the image that you portray. A strong portfolio will bring you more jobs, more money, and more pictures to add to your portfolio to give that well-rounded representation of yourself.

WEBFOLIO

Webfolios are great when first starting out as they allow you to show your portfolio to clients, agencies and portfolios with minimal effort and they are quick to update. Along with this they offer a model the chance to include more images and present a wider range of their talents and looks, whilst also providing all necessary information (age, contact information, and statistics) all within the same space, at just the click of a button.

Z-CARDS

Sometimes model jargon can be difficult to understand when you are not used to the terms; Z-cards are effectively models' business cards. A Z-card should display your statistics, contact information, and a variety of portfolio images, including one headshot, one natural shot, and a selection of your best images.

A Z-card is used as a standard in the industry as a way to advertise yourself and is often a more convenient way to leave a sample of your portfolio with clients. It's always advisable to carry Z-cards with you, as you never know when you will meet a potential contact.

CHAPTER 19

❖

Staying Safe

I would like to discuss the topic of safety, specifically for models and the dangers they could potentially face, alongside some basic safety advice when using sites such as Model Mayhem.

This advice is by no means a foolproof guide to avoiding potentially dangerous people or situations after booking shoots online. Nothing is ever guaranteed, and life is constantly full of surprises and risks.

However, I hope this advice is circulated and passed on to new and aspiring models to help keep them a little bit safer and open their eyes to the potential dangers and pitfalls an inexperienced person could face when entering the modelling industry. Additionally, I hope it gives them a few skills to exercise in order to avoid certain unsavoury individuals and situations.

As a new model, you will be an easier target, and to keep oneself as safe as possible is an absolute necessity. I hope everyone reading this article will pass this information along and comment with other ideas and tips.

Safety should be number one on your list of priorities.

***Tip – Take a friend or family member with you to the shoot. They can sit on a sofa and watch.

I would advise asking your agency for advice and what precautions they take when booking you for jobs.

Below are my personal top tips for staying safe:

- I always leave information of your whereabouts with someone close to me such as friend, parents, partner it should be someone who will notice if i don't check in when agreed. I always include the name and phone number, as well as the shoot address, of the person with whom you will be working.

- I make sure someone knows when i'm expected back from the shoot. It is a good idea to notify someone when you arrive at a shoot and when you leave and get home safely.

- If you are flying out of the country, leave the flight number, times, and dates, as well as any hotel information, with someone at home and let them know when you will be arriving and leaving, and by when to expect to hear from you.

- I always make sure my phone is fully charged.

- I take 2 external mobile phone batteries

- I text the make, model, and licence plate of the car belonging to the person im working with.

- Take Cash/working debit or credit card, in case you need to grab a taxi at any stage or get out of a given situation.

- Take my own water with you, or only accept drinks that are clearly still sealed or straight from a tap.

- I never drink alcohol at shoots.

- Carry painkillers with you in case of headaches or menstrual cramps. It is better to not take prescription or over-the-counter drugs from people you do not know

- Most of the time i take someone with me, even if i have to pay their travel costs.

The number of models now available has increased a thousandfold due to the internet. Sites like Model Mayhem attract millions of people from all around the world.

The same goes for photographers. DSLR cameras are now readily available at reasonable prices to anyone. Therefore, many more people now supplement their income, and/or have a creative outlet, through photography than in the past.

The result of these two issues combined has meant that the number of potential issues with safety has also increased.

Primarily, your safety should be your priority – no job is EVER worth compromising your safety for. Due to the fact that the internet has meant you do not have proof of whom you are talking to, I recommend you do book work online that you check out who you are looking at working with before you agree to a shoot. If you have reservations, do not agree to the shoot in the first place.

Do this by checking with other models how the person is to work with, and always ask the photographer for references so he or she knows you will be checking on them and their professionalism.

I cannot stress enough that if you do book a shoot with someone, and you do feel after getting there that you made a mistake, NEVER be too scared to walk out. Always make sure you have the means to leave in case of emergencies.

❖

CHAPTER 20

Child Modelling

C hild models tend to be between two and twelve years of age, and it is much more widely accepted in this area of the industry that a diverse selection is desired. The requirements that you would find in other areas of modelling like weight, size, and height are much more variable, and what agencies look for above all else is a confident, happy, and compatible child with an attractive look.

The regulation of child modelling is obviously and rightly stricter than other areas of modelling. The key objective is to ensure that no detriment is caused to the child's educational development and to safeguard against exploitation.

In order for a child under the age of 16 to work, the parent or guardian must hold a licence and abide by the strict guidelines around length of shoot and number of working hours. In addition to this, all reputable modelling agencies will insist that a biological parent or legal guardian is present at any shoot.

In recent years there has been a measurable surge in the marketability of children's clothing, and many major fashion houses have branched out into this profitable enterprise. This has meant that the need for child models has increased, and there are now multiple areas available to child models, including catalogue, advertising, and high-street fashion, and work as TV and film extras.

In the child modelling category, there is always a demand for new models, as there is a large variety of media requiring a vast selection of models. Work can include catalogues, hotel brochures, furniture commercials, and food advertisements, to name but a few.

Sending off an application is something that, as a parent, you should understandably think hard about.

Child models must be confident and enjoy being in front of the camera. This isn't always easy to decide until your child has been involved in a professional photo-shoot environment.

There are strict guidelines for the amount of hours models can work and any model under the age of 16 must have a licence to work. These restrictions are in place to guarantee your child is not overworked and that schooling always comes first. A parent or guardian is always required to attend shoots with the model and should act as their manager, as they will always put their child's needs first.

YOU CAN APPLY FOR A PERFORMANCE LICENCE AT THE FOLLOWING LINK:

https://www.gov.uk/apply-for-child-performance-licence

How much your child will earn doing modelling?

Well, this is an impossible question to answer, as with adult modelling many factors come into play. Firstly, your agency does not decide how much you get paid per job so there is no point in trying to push them to give you more money. They can only pay you what the client offers per job (the client is the brand).

It will vary from job to job, and there is no hard and fast rule. However, know this – if your agency is taking 20% of your earnings, this is a great thing as you know they will be pushing to get you as many jobs as possible and also the best-paid jobs!

THE MORE MONEY YOU MAKE, THE MORE MONEY THEY MAKE!

I believe it important that as the child's parent or guardian you take full responsibility as their manager.

At the end of the day, no one is going to be more reliable than you (the parent/guardian) in assuring your child's best interests are at the forefront of all decisions, and the journey of a modelling career can lead to the relationship that you and your child share flourishing.

CHAPTER 21

Staying Safe

Successful modelling isn't just about how well clothes fit a model. Models must have a look that's relatable and speaks to their target audience. However, as not all brands have the same clients, it's the model's responsibility to ensure that their look is adaptable and versatile.

One of the ways versatility can be accomplished is through posing. Depending on the brand, the way a model poses varies drastically. For example, models posing for a Gucci campaign portray a much different creative vision than those posing for M&S.

When it comes to posing, it's important to stay inspired! Even top models continue practicing their poses so they stay current. Gathering inspiration can be done in multiple ways.

YouTube Videos

In current times, YouTube is a great way to look at what is happening in the industry right now. There is loads videos online talking about some of the basic poses that models use. i would suggest practicing these first. Once you have an understanding of the basic poses, you can start building on to them.

HERE IS SOME EXAMPLES

https://www.youtube.com/watch?v=mWRzgc2t4vY&t=29s

https://www.youtube.com/watch?v=UQePS1HEtHE&t=46s

https://www.youtube.com/watch?v=cPv_b-th13M

MAGAZINE EDITORIALS

Fashion magazines are fantastic ways to gather inspiration. Here you can assess the way different brands have their models pose in order to sell their specific products. As the top fashion brands advertise in magazines, models are able to see the unique and creative ways fashion models use their body to successfully capture a creative vision. Especially during new fashion clothing seasons, brands are constantly changing their ads and thus giving aspiring models more ideas to recreate.

OTHER MODELS

One great tool for perfecting posing is speaking to other models. Find out if they have tricks and tips for capturing a certain look. While poses might be similar they may do something slightly different that you didn't previously think of. Listen closely and ask them to show you any go-to poses they have up their sleeve.

❖

CHAPTER 22

Successful modelling isn't just about how well clothes fit a model. Models must have a look that's relatable and speaks to their target audience. However, as not all brands have the same clients, it's the model's responsibility to ensure that their look is adaptable and versatile.

One of the ways versatility can be accomplished is through posing. Depending on the brand, the way a model poses varies drastically. For example, models posing for a Gucci campaign portray a much different creative vision than those posing for M&S.

When it comes to posing, it's important to stay inspired! Even top models continue practicing their poses so they stay current. Gathering inspiration can be done in multiple ways.

YOUTUBE VIDEOS

In current times, YouTube is a great way to look at what is happening in the industry right now. There is loads videos online talking about some of the basic poses that models use. i would suggest practicing these first. Once you have an understanding of the basic poses, you can start building on to them.

HERE IS SOME EXAMPLES

https://www.youtube.com/watch?v=mWRzgc2t4vY&t=29s

https://www.youtube.com/watch?v=UQePS1HEtHE&t=46s

https://www.youtube.com/watch?v=cPv_b-th13M

MAGAZINE EDITORIALS

Fashion magazines are fantastic ways to gather inspiration. Here you can assess the way different brands have their models pose in order to sell their specific products. As the top fashion brands advertise in magazines, models are able to see the unique and creative ways fashion models use their body to successfully capture a creative vision. Especially during new fashion clothing seasons, brands are constantly changing their ads and thus giving aspiring models more ideas to recreate.

OTHER MODELS

One great tool for perfecting posing is speaking to other models. Find out if they have tricks and tips for capturing a certain look. While poses might be similar they may do something slightly different that you didn't previously think of. Listen closely and ask them to show you any go-to poses they have up their sleeve.

❖

CHAPTER 23

Modelling Scams

As you will have no doubt heard by now there are some rogue modelling agencies around.

The key to avoiding modelling scams, in my opinion, is to work with agencies who work on a commission basis, meaning every time you get a paid job, they get paid.

Modelling agencies in the UK are not allowed to charge an upfront joining fee. However, this does not mean they will pay for your portfolio. You will generally need to cover the cost of this yourself.

Talent companies can charge upfront fees, and many do charge a small one, normally between £60–£180 a year. This is quite normal, and if it happens you could ask them to refund it after your first job. Many companies would be happy to do this, as it would also show a commitment from yourself.

CHAPTER 24

Your Reputation

Your agent needs to know they can rely on you and that you are committed. Having worked with three of the UK's largest modelling platforms, I know what agencies and platforms want from models. Here are the top tips for creating your modelling personality:

- Make sure you turn up fresh and prepared for every job.

- Read the brief.

- Ask questions about the job before you say 'Yes', not after, as it looks unprofessional and agents may worry that you will change your mind in future, which makes them look bad.

- Turn up to the job on time or, even better, 20 minutes early.

- Your agency will normally contact you via email or text message. Reply within an appropriate time frame. I recommend four hours max.

- When shooting for fashion brands, take care with the equipment, props, clothes, etc.

- Research the brand before you accept the job.

- Act professionally while on set. Even top models like Kate Moss and Naomi Campbell are expected to create a good impression while on set.

- Treat everyone on set and at the agency with respect.

- Do not accept a job unless you are 100% sure you are going to be able to do it!

❖

CHAPTER 25

Patience is a virtue

When you start modelling you will be hoping and expecting that everything will happen very quickly. This is rarely the case. Many models wait months to get signed to an agency and then months more to get their first job.

Some are very lucky and find it happens within days and weeks, and if this is you, great. However, this will normally be the case only for around ten per cent of the people trying to break into the industry. In my experience, for the rest of us, it takes time, hard work, and perseverance, so the key is to keep at it and not give up at the first hurdle.

CHAPTER 26

What Next?

Well this is where i leave you however feel free to reach out to me on my website http://themodel-coach.online/ or look me up on instagram im always happy to help models and hear feedback on my books i have a range of 5 modelling books which cover every aspect of the industry.

What next for you? Well if you want my advice you should start by making a plan get a notepad and start with the 5 W's fill one page for each W

Where - *are you going to market yourself*

When - *When will you start and how much time each week will you dedicate to succeeding*

Why - *you want to do this*

Who - *what contacts you need to make*

What - *you hope to achieve*

HOW ARE YOU GOING TO MAKE ALL THIS HAPPEN...

❖

CHAPTER 27

Example Introduction Letter

Name

Address

Mobile

Email

Dear _____,

I am writing to apply for a modelling position with your agency. I have photo-shoot experience of modelling in various locations with multiple looks. My versatility allows me to work within different modelling sectors. Additionally, my confidence in front of the camera is evident in my photos. I am a motivated individual, who strives to maintain a positive attitude during every photo shoot. I am a strong team player who listens closely and takes direction easily.

I would love to meet in person to demonstrate my strengths and prove I am an excellent fit for this position. Please do not hesitate to get in contact with me by phone or email.

Thank you for your time, and I look forward to hearing from you.

Your Sincerely

48762131R00052

Printed in Poland
by Amazon Fulfillment
Poland Sp. z o.o., Wrocław